Congratulations on making one of the be
of your life, your own education. **You are**
limited by your imagination and the 1
exercises and life choice options in th
will make every aspect of your life bet

Your body is designed to move for optimal performance. The healthiest people in the world do not go to gyms but incorporate physical activity into their daily routines. Thousands of studies have shown the benefits of regular physical activity.

Body weight training may look easy, but if you're not used to it or make subtle variations at can be extremely challenging. If you struggle at the start it is OK and even expected, **leave your ego at the door.** Do routines at your own pace and take longer breaks if you need it.

Exercise intensity is key for optimal benefits and should be modified on a case by case basis. Challenge yourself and **set goals**. If you are new to body weight training start on level 1 (novice), and remember we are all novices at some point. **Focus on your goals:** weight loss, muscle gain, strength gain, looking better naked ☺ or just looking to have fun, this text can help with it all.

The routines in the book are safe for all age groups and gender variations, all physical abilities can benefit from regular activity routines. **Know your limit, and play within it** - stop exercise if you experience unexpected pain, discomfort or severe shortness of breath and consult your local healthcare provider.

pots or sheets and even kids ☺). Access to a pull-up bar or monkey bars, could also be of benefit.

Workout routines are **read left to right** with the number of reps, sets and rest time are determined based on fitness level and training goals.

1. **Level 1 (novice) - 2 minutes rest**
2. **Level 2 (intermediate) - 60 sec rest**
3. **Level 3 (advanced) - 20 second rest**

The exercises selected **should be modified to meet and gently challenge your current abilities**; can't do a push-up? - no problem, do it with your knees on the ground or a wall push-up. Push-ups are too easy for you? - put your feet up on a chair or load a back pack full of books and see how you do. **Move slower for more resistance.**

Of utmost importance is your motivation - **Why do you want to do this and what are your goals?** - Write them down here, and refer back often:

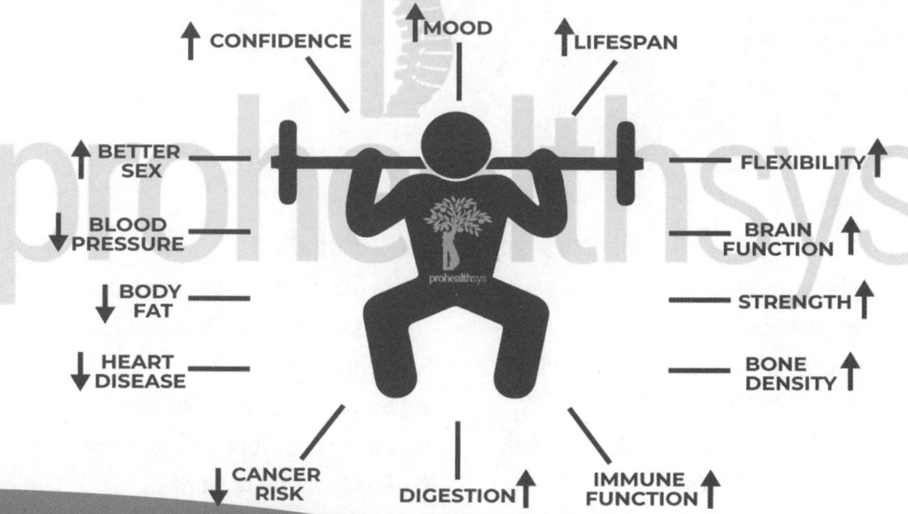

Introduction Health

Scientists generally recognize five determinants of health:

Individual behavior - Yours to Control!

- **Diet** (eat whole, unprocessed foods)
- **Physical activity** (just do it!) - According to the world health organization Physical Inactivity is the 4th leading cause of global mortality
- **Sleep** (this is where you recover)
- Poor 'foods,' alcohol, cigarette & drugs

Genetics and biology

- **Age** (you can be physiologically younger by the choices you make)
- Gender & Inherited conditions (genetics)

Social determinants

- Availability of resources to meet daily needs (education, jobs, real foods)
- Exposure to crime, violence, and social disorder (eg. trash or discrimination)
- Transportation options & public safety

Environment determinants

- Natural environment (plants, forests, weather, climate, light and pets)
- Built environment (buildings, workstation ergonomics, transportation)
- Toxic substances, physical hazards and barriers (esp. for disabled individuals)

Health services determinants

- Both **access and quality are key**
- Lack of **good quality** availability
- Limited language access, high cost

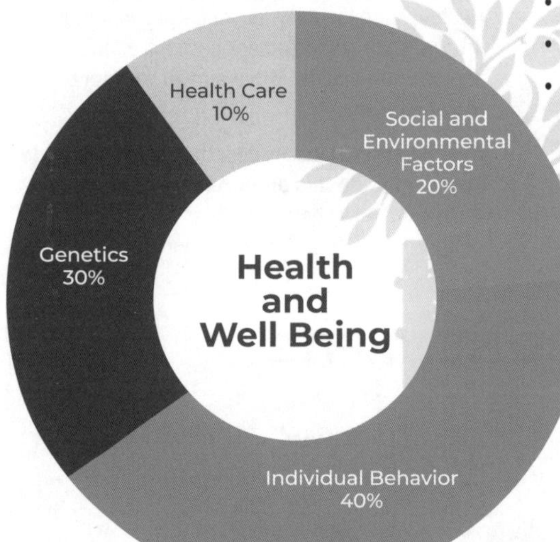

You can control your behavior, healthcare and many social/environmental factors and can influence your genetic expression

Factors that IMPROVE healing

1. **Laughter, positive mood & good sleep**
2. **Love, community & social support**
3. **Adequate nutrition (food is medicine) - whole unprocessed foods**
4. **Younger physiologic age** (life choices)
5. **Good blood supply** (nutrient/waste exchange)
6. **Aerobic fitness, activity & movement**
7. **Massage & Joint Mobilizations**
8. **Acupuncture**
9. **Surgical interventions** (last resort)
10. **Lower toxic load (environmental & social)**
11. **Positive expectations**

Introduction Health

Things You Can Control

Your Gratitude

Your Physique

Your Habits

Your Network

Your Work Rate

Your Attitude

Your attitude determines your altitude.

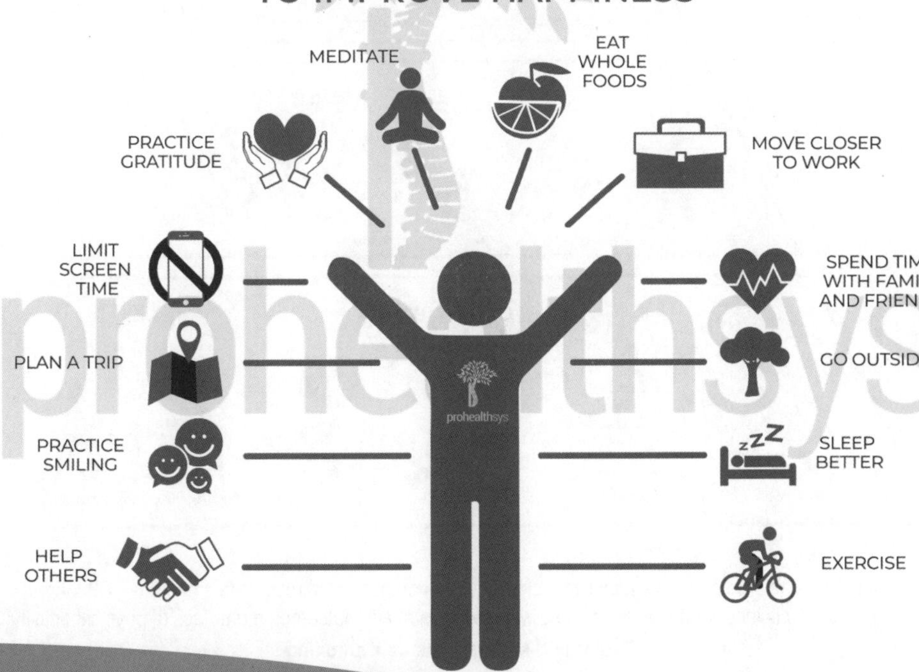

Intro Health

The world's healthiest people don't go to the gym, they make walking and physical activity a part of their regular day. The American Cancer Society, researchers have found that walking for six hours per week can help one live longer and reduced your lifetime risk of cancer. A study from Harvard Medical School, walking reduces the risk of cardiovascular diseases by 31% and risk of dying from it by 32%, and reduce your risk of dementia by ~40%.

People in the world's Blue Zones (the places around the world with the highest life expectancy) don't pump iron, run marathons or join gyms. Studies have determined that **routine natural movement** is one of the best ways to increase your life span. Research shows that the best work commute you can have is a 15-minute walk each way, but any physical activity in your commute is a win (#takethestairs).

Limit screen time
(TV, computer, tablet & phone) - there are rehab centers dedicated to help reduce this addiction many people have ...

Limit all screen time and have consistent changes of body position through the entire day - Prolonged sedentary time is independently associated with negative health outcomes regardless of physical activity!

Prolonged sitting is the new smoking

(Aviroop, B. et. al. Sedentary Time and Its Association With Risk for Disease Incidence, Mortality, and Hospitalization in Adults: A Systematic Review and Meta-analysis. Annals of Internal Medicine. Jan, 2015.)

Dangers of Prolonged Sitting

WAYS TO INCREASE MOVEMENT AT WORK

Standing meetings
Stand or walk during meetings to improve engagement

Work standing, burns 40% more calories than sitting

Talk in person
Talk to co-workers rather then text or email

Walking break, whenever possible eat lunch out of office

Move
Squat at your desk
Use your big muscles to improve health

Water
Stay hydrated, walk to the bathroom

Walk around when talking on the phone

Stretch & Move every 45 min at your desk

Training Terminology

Sets and Reps

Rep (repetition) = 1 complete movement

Set = number of times a group of reps is done

Total volume = reps x sets x weight

For strength, studies show that the most important factor is the intensity. The harder you try to failure, the stronger you become.

ProTip: a commonly ignored yet incredibly useful strategy is to record yourself with your smart phone doing a specific exercise so you can actually SEE your form vs. tracking it mentally. Beyond basic you can also see changes over time that can be very inspiring! **Use a fitness diary to track changes in performance.**

Superset - 2 exercises done back to back without any rest between them

Drop set - at the end of your set, drop weight 15-20% and perform reps to failure

Rest Pause - after a set, rest 15 seconds, go again to failure, rest another 15 sec & repeat

Alternate sets - pair exercises for opposing muscle groups and alternate between sets

AMRAP - doing "as many reps as possible"

DOMS - delayed onset muscular soreness. Soreness after doing a new exercise or activity.

Compound - exercise that uncovers more than one joint or muscle group

Isolation - exercise that involves one joint and focuses on one muscle group

EMOM - performing a given number of reps "every minute on the minute"

Negatives - focusing on the **eccentric** or lengthening muscle contraction. Eg downward part of a bicep curl

Progressive overload - gradual increase of stress put in body (increase of weight/speed/volume)

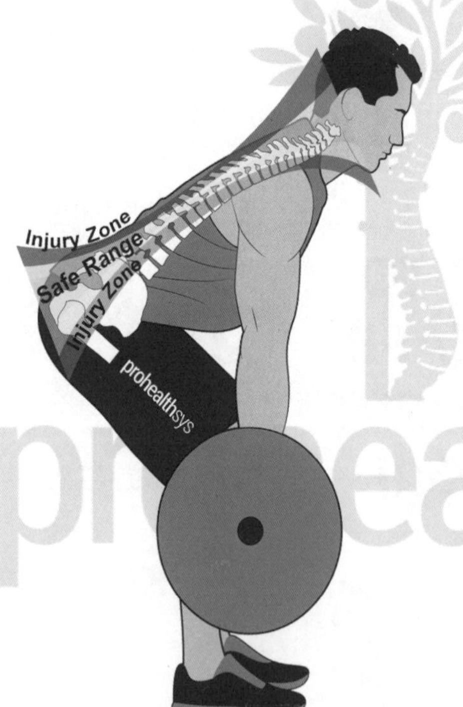

Reps	Training Goal
2	
3	
4	**STRENGTH** (3-5 sets, 3-5 reps)
5	
6	
7	
8	
9	
10	**HYPERTROPHY** (3-4 sets, 8-12 reps)
11	
12	
13	
14	
15	
16	**ENDURANCE** (1-2 sets, 15+ reps)
17	
18+	

Training Terminology

Workout Intensity

It is NOT heavy weights that matter, it is perceived effort (intensity). Low loads with high volumes can be as effective as heavy loads at low volumes. **Training with a high level of effort is the most important thing**. Intensity requires **visualization and metal focus for optimization.**

1. Have a plan and minimize distractions (no phones).
2. Have **pure mental focus** on maintaining proper form and safely pushing limits. Find NEW limits by doing an extra rep when you feel done.
3. Your true goal is to give each set everything you've got and reach muscle failure. If you feel tired, force yourself to PUSH through.

There are 2 main measures of intensity:

1. **Heart rate** (HR_{max}) - beats per minute
2. **Rate of Perceived Exertions** (RPE)

Gauging Intensity using Heart Rate (HR) - the basic way to calculate maximum heart rate is to **subtract age from 220**.

220 - 40 yrs old = 180 beats/min max

- **Moderate intensity: 50-70% max HR**
- **Vigorous intensity: 70-85% max HR**

Exercise prescription - get F I T T

Frequency: __ x wk - find a balance between enough stress for tissue growth, healing and adaptation.

Intensity: effort during exercise (% of max). Balance intensity hard enough to overload the body but not so difficult that it results in overtraining, injury or burnout.

Time: how long each session should last. Varies based on the intensity and type.

Type: cardiovascular, strength and flexibility training. Based on goals & specific exercises performed

Cardiovascular training

3-5 x week, 60-85% 1 rep max, 20-60 min

Strength training

2-3x wk, 70-90% 1 rep max, 8-10 reps, 1-3 sets

Flexibility training

2-3x wk, 10-30 sec holds, 2-4 reps (yoga)

adapted from ACSM (American College of Sport Medicine)

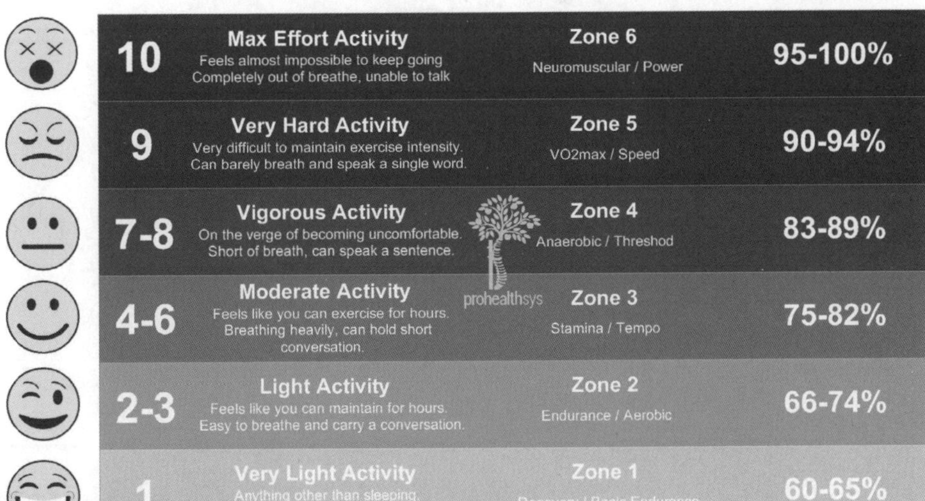

RPE Chart (Rate of Perceived Exertion)		Training Zone	% Maximum Heart Rate
10	**Max Effort Activity** Feels almost impossible to keep going. Completely out of breathe, unable to talk	Zone 6 Neuromuscular / Power	95-100%
9	**Very Hard Activity** Very difficult to maintain exercise intensity. Can barely breath and speak a single word.	Zone 5 VO2max / Speed	90-94%
7-8	**Vigorous Activity** On the verge of becoming uncomfortable. Short of breath, can speak a sentence.	Zone 4 Anaerobic / Threshod	83-89%
4-6	**Moderate Activity** Feels like you can exercise for hours. Breathing heavily, can hold short conversation.	Zone 3 Stamina / Tempo	75-82%
2-3	**Light Activity** Feels like you can maintain for hours. Easy to breathe and carry a conversation.	Zone 2 Endurance / Aerobic	66-74%
1	**Very Light Activity** Anything other than sleeping, watching TV, riding in a car, etc.	Zone 1 Recovery / Basic Endurance	60-65%

Training Goals

HOW MANY REPS
SHOULD YOU DO?

STRENGTH
HYPERTROPHY
ENDURANCE
HYPERTROPHY
STRENGTH
ENDURANCE
ENDURANCE
HYPERTROPHY
STRENGTH
prohealthsys
№ OF REPS
1
5
10
15
STRENGTH: 1-5
HYPERTROPHY: 6-12
ENDURANCE: 13-20

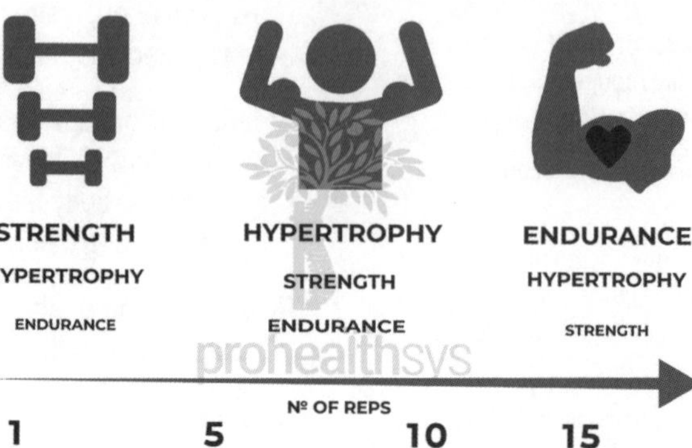

MUSCLE BUILDING

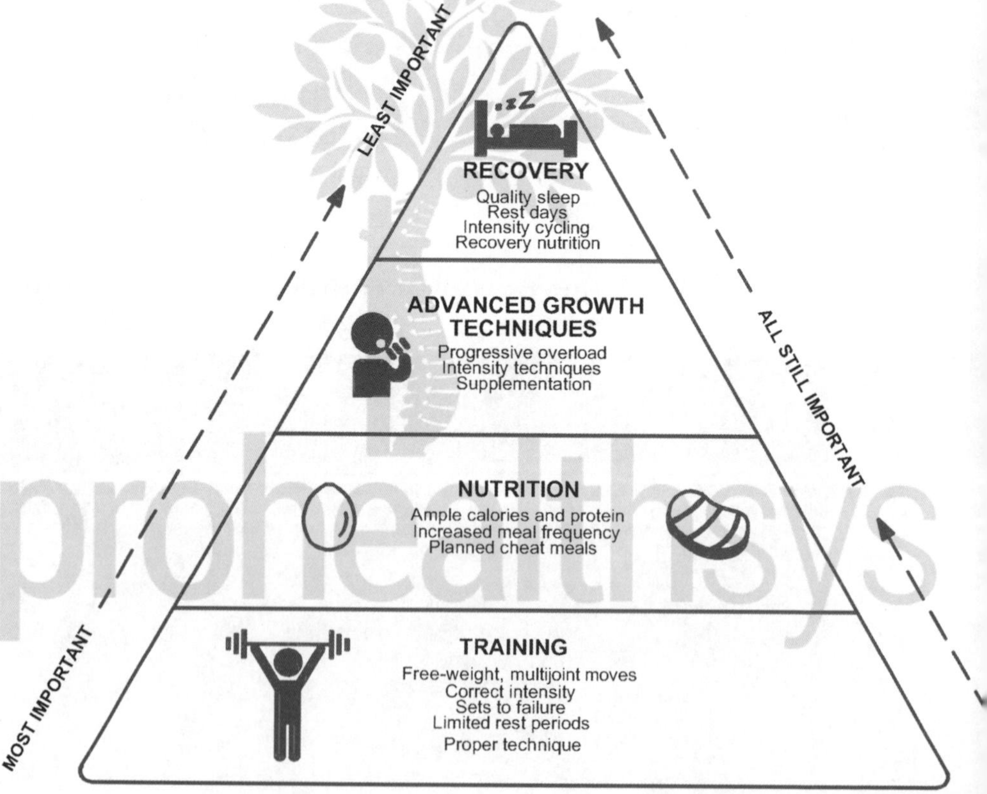

LEAST IMPORTANT
MOST IMPORTANT
ALL STILL IMPORTANT
RECOVERY
Quality sleep
Rest days
Intensity cycling
Recovery nutrition
ADVANCED GROWTH TECHNIQUES
Progressive overload
Intensity techniques
Supplementation
NUTRITION
Ample calories and protein
Increased meal frequency
Planned cheat meals
TRAINING
Free-weight, multijoint moves
Correct intensity
Sets to failure
Limited rest periods
Proper technique

Training Goals

THE TRUTH ABOUT
FAT LOSS
STRENGTH 10%
DIET 15%
CARDIO 75%
WHAT MOST PEOPLE END UP DOING
STRENGTH 15%
CARDIO 10%
DIET 75%
WHAT YOU SHOULD BE DOING
prohealthsys

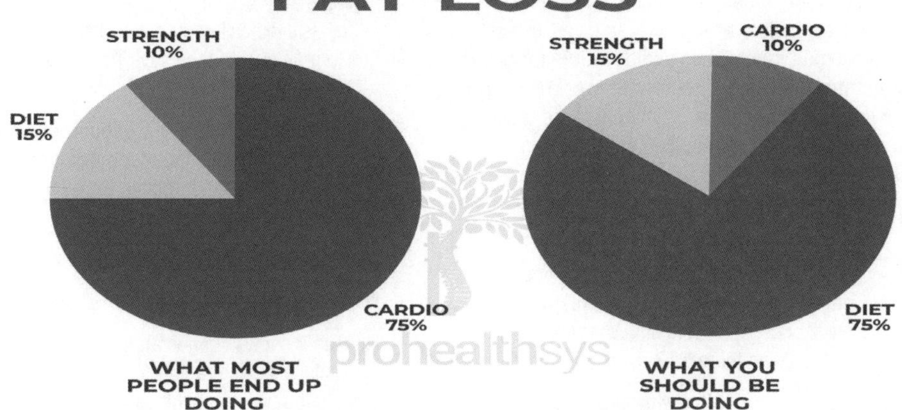

FAT LOSS
LEAST IMPORTANT
MOST IMPORTANT
ALL STILL IMPORTANT
CARDIO
great for mental clarity
SLEEP
7-9 hours/night
keeps your hunger levels in check,
allows you to properly recover/recharge
LIFTING WEIGHTS
2-5x per week
focus on getting stronger over time
30-60 min sessions
PROTEIN INTAKE
consume 7g-1g per pound of bodyweight
the rest of your calories can come from whatever combo
of carbs and fats you prefer
CALORIE DEFICIT
cause it's the only way to lose fat
start by multiplying current bodyweight by 10-12
adjust if necessary, recalculate every 2-4 weeks as you lose weight
prohealthsys

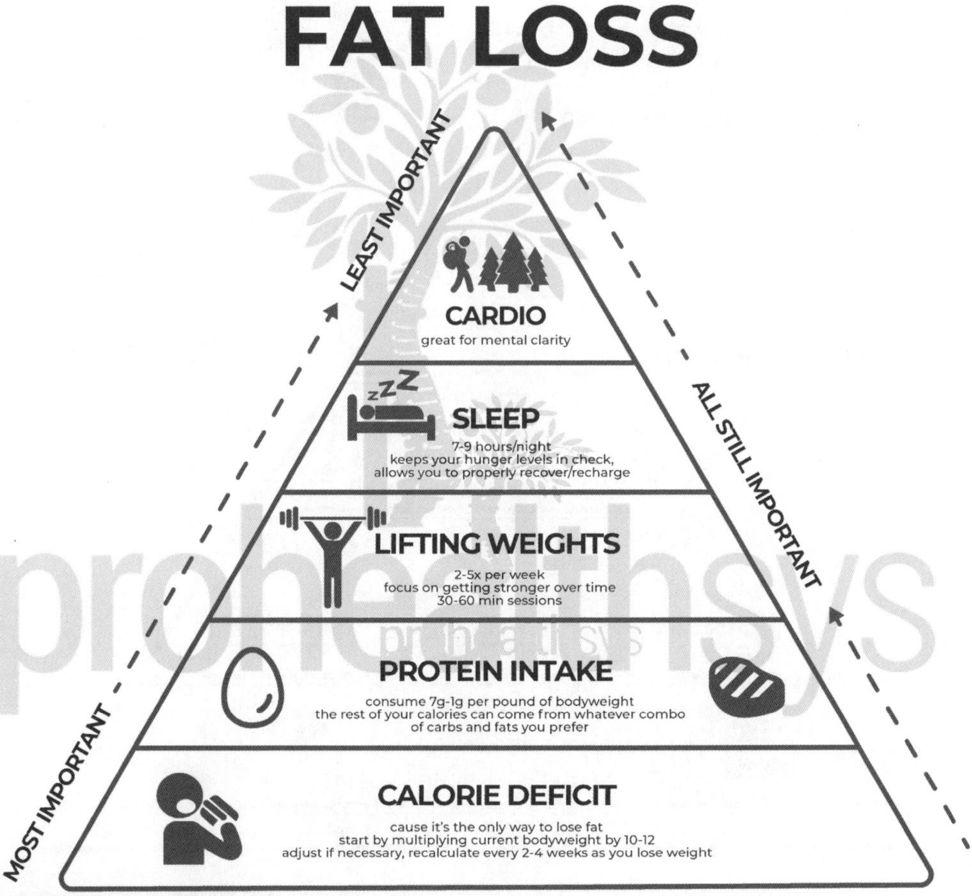

Nutrition

Respected food writer Michael Pollan says everything he's learned about food and health can be summed up in seven words: **"Eat food, not too much, mostly plants."** Eat real food -- vegetables, fruits, whole grains, and, yes, fish and natural organic meats and **avoid "edible food-like substances."** There is no need to over complicate the science, the hard part is sticking to the regime and finding good food sources. Here are some words of advice:

1. **Don't eat anything your great grand parents wouldn't recognize as food.** "When you pick up that box of cookies, or eat something with 15 ingredients you can't pronounce, ask yourself, "What are those things doing there?"
2. **Don't eat anything with more than 5 ingredients, or ingredients you can't pronounce.**
3. Bacteria eat real food, so should you. **Don't eat anything that won't eventually rot.** "There are exceptions -- honey -- but as a rule, things like Twinkies that never go bad aren't food."
4. **Always leave the table a little hungry**," Pollan says. "Many cultures have rules that you stop eating before you are full. In Japan, they say eat until you are four-fifths full. Islamic culture has a similar rule, and in German culture they say, 'Tie off the sack before it's full.'"
5. **Families traditionally ate together, around a table and not a TV, at regular meal times.** It's a good tradition. **Enjoy meals with the people you love.**

Nutrition & Feeding Window

- **"Feeding window" = within 1 hr after class**
- Research shows, immediately after workout insulin levels spike rapidly for a few hours priming the body for synthesizing new muscle, limiting exercise-induced muscle loss, and restoring energy levels - consuming **20-40g of protein within 2 hrs following workout significantly increases muscle growth**

1. Stark M, Lukaszuk J, Prawitz A, Salacinski A. Protein timing and its effects on muscular hypertrophy and strength in individuals engaged in weight-training. Journal of the International Society of Sports Nutrition. 2012;9:54. doi:10.1186/1550-2783-9-54.
2. Kerksick C, Harvey T, Stout J, Campbell B, Wilborn C, Kreider R, Kalman D, Ziegenfuss T, Lopez H, Landis J, Ivy JL, Antonio J: International Society of Sports Nutrition position stand: nutrient timing. J Int Soc Sports Nutr. 2008, 5: 17-10.1186/1550-2783-5-17.

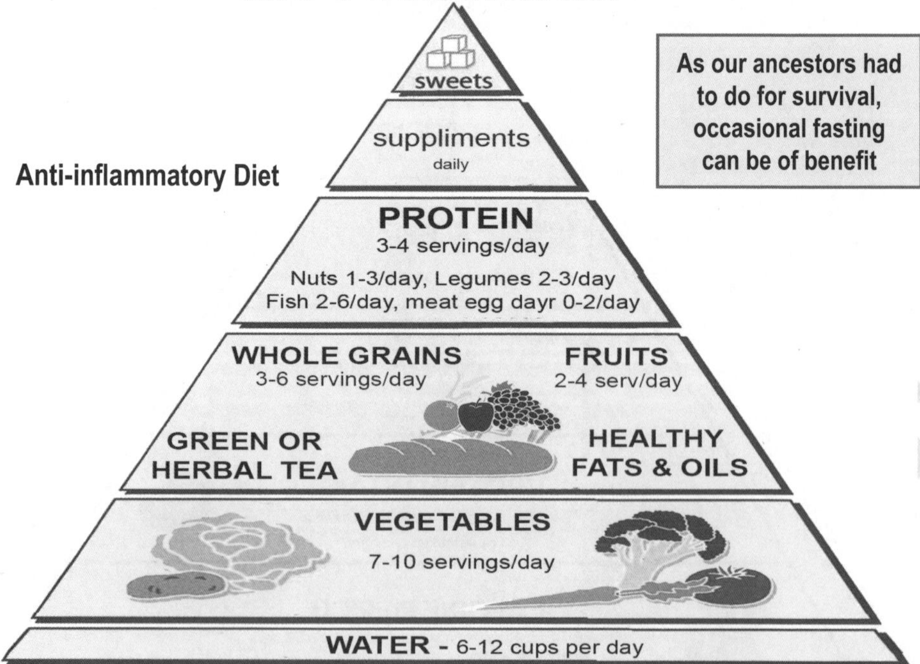

'Those who think they have no time for healthy eating...will sooner or later have to find time for illness.' - Edward Stanley

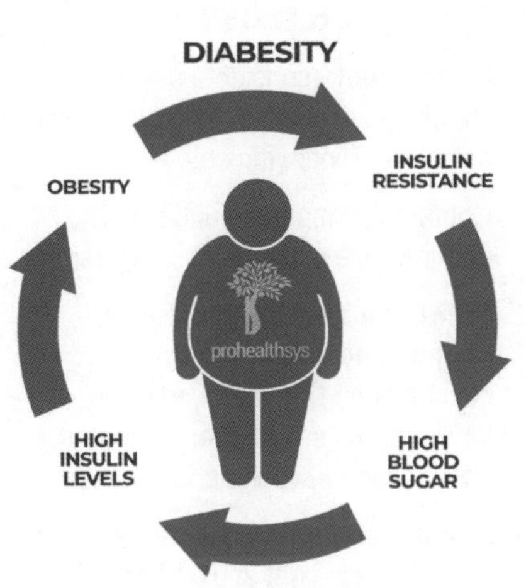

Eat less CRAP:

 C - carbonated drinks

 R - refined sugar

 A - artificial sweeteners

 P - processed foods

Eat more FOOD:

 F - fruits & veggies

 O - organic lean proteins

 O - omega 3 fatty acids

 D - drink water

EVERY BITE YOU TAKE IS EITHER

FIGHTING DISEASE OR FEEDING IT

Sleep

Sleep is when you recover physically and mentally. Healthy sleep habits can make a huge difference in your quality of life. Sleep benefits include:

1. Improved mood and function
2. Better maintenance of body weight (yes you can burn fat in your sleep)
3. Improved immune function
4. Look more attractive
5. Lower risk of injury

Practice a relaxing bedtime ritual away from bright lights. A relaxing routine helps separate your sleep time from activities that can cause excitement, stress or anxiety which can make it more difficult to fall asleep. Spend the last hour before bed doing a calming activity such as reading. **Avoid electronics before bed or in the middle of the night.**

"Remove electrons from your room"

Exercise daily. Vigorous exercise is best, but even light exercise is better than no activity. Exercise at any time of day, but not at the expense of your sleep.

Bedroom Setup

- Temperature cool ~18°C (60°F)
- **Quiet & dark** (consider using blackout curtains, eye shades, ear plugs, "white noise" machines, fans etc.)
- Comfortable mattress and pillows (mattress life expectancy ~10 years)
- **No work materials, computers, phones and TVs** in sleeping environment. Use your bed only for sleep and sex to strengthen the association between bed and sleep.

See the Morning Light. Your body's internal clock is sensitive to light and darkness, so getting a dose of the sun first thing in the morning will help you wake up. **Avoid bright light in the evening, especially blue light.** This will keep your circadian rhythms in check.

It's not just what you eat—it's when you eat. While you know that it's not a good idea to go to bed on an empty stomach, being stuffed is just as bad. **Avoid alcohol, cigarettes, and heavy meals in the evening**. Avoid eating large meals for two to three hours before bedtime. Try a light snack 45 minutes before bed if you're still hungry.

5 Ways to Improve Your Sleep

Get up at the same time every day

Get 15-30 minutes of sunlight each morning

Do relaxing activities before bed

Use your bedroom only for sleep and sex

Avoid screen light, caffeine, and alcohol before bed

Sleep

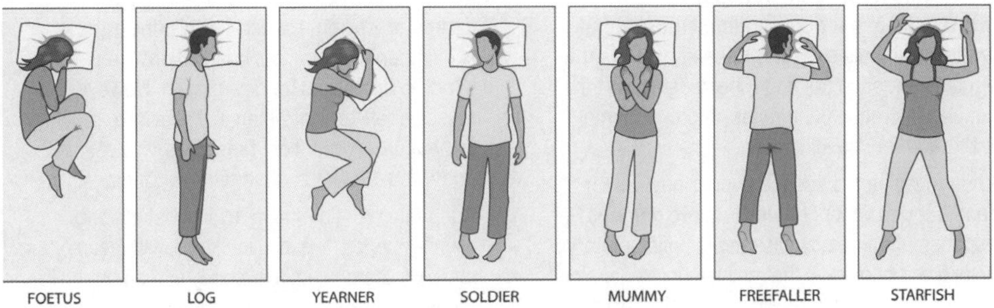

FOETUS
LOG
YEARNER
SOLDIER
MUMMY
FREEFALLER
STARFISH

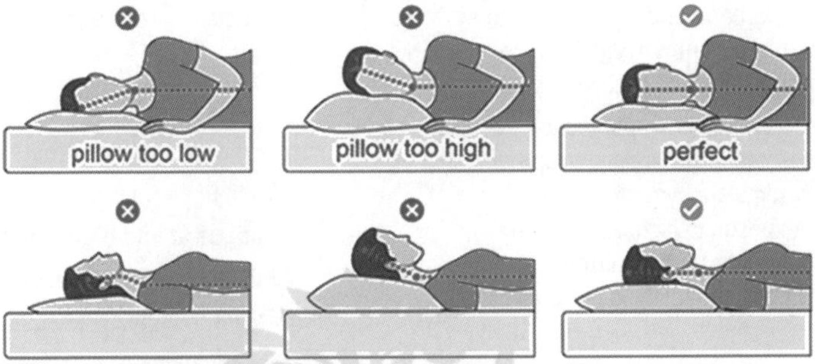

pillow too low
pillow too high
perfect

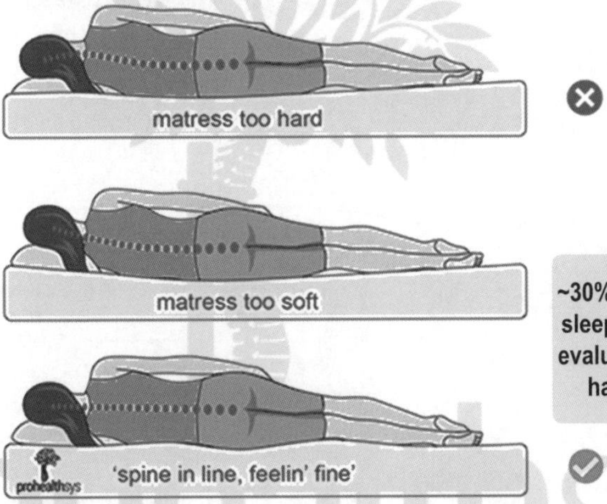

matress too hard
matress too soft
prohealthsys
'spine in line, feelin' fine'

~30% of our life is spent sleeping. It is crucial to evaluate sleep systems, habits & positions

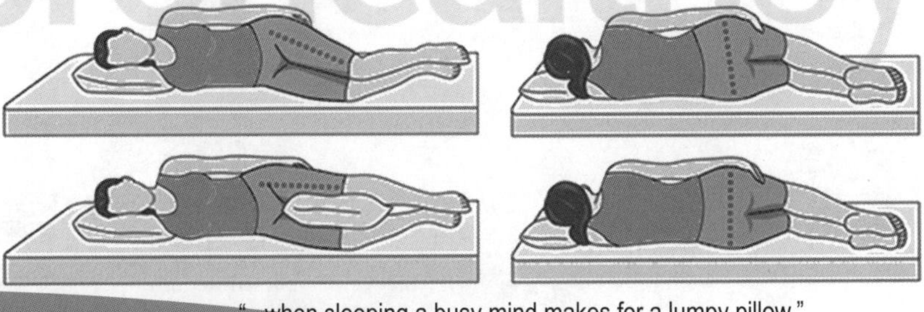

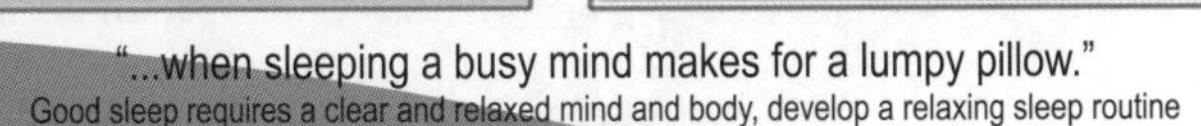

"...when sleeping a busy mind makes for a lumpy pillow."

Good sleep requires a clear and relaxed mind and body, develop a relaxing sleep routine

Training Effect

Resistance training is gradually & progressively overloading musculoskeletal system so it gets stronger. Research shows that regular resistance training will strengthen & tone muscles, increase bone mass, improve mental health and reduce injury risk.

When muscles are stressed under heavier loads, they experience **microscopic damage**; in response, the injured cells release inflammatory molecules (cytokines) that activate injury repair. The greater the damage to the muscle tissue, the more your body will need to repair itself . The resulting **cycle of damage and repair eventually makes muscles bigger and stronger** as they adapt to progressive demands (training effect).

Since our bodies have already adapted to most everyday activities, those generally don't produce enough stress to stimulate hypertrophy, our cells need to be exposed to higher or different workloads. **Atrophy occurs if you don't continuously expose muscles to resistance**.

In contrast, exposing the muscle to a high degree of tension, especially while the muscle is lengthening (eccentric contraction), generates effective conditions for new growth. However, muscles rely on more than just activity to grow without proper nutrition, hormones, and rest your body would never be able to repair damage.

Adequate protein (amino acids) intake along with hormones, like insulin-like growth factor and testosterone, shift the body into an anabolic (growth) state. This repair process mainly occurs when we're resting, especially while sleeping. Repair is affected by rest, age, gender & genetics.

Signs of Over Training

1. **Increased injury rate - greatest with:**
   - **Lack of warm up**
   - **Fatigue at end of activity**
   - **Full eccentric to concentric action**
2. **Persistent muscle soreness**
3. **Increased susceptibility to infections**
4. **Irritability, depression, insomnia**
5. **Loss of motivation, libido, menstruation**
6. **Halted progress (or regression)**
7. **Altered resting heart rate**

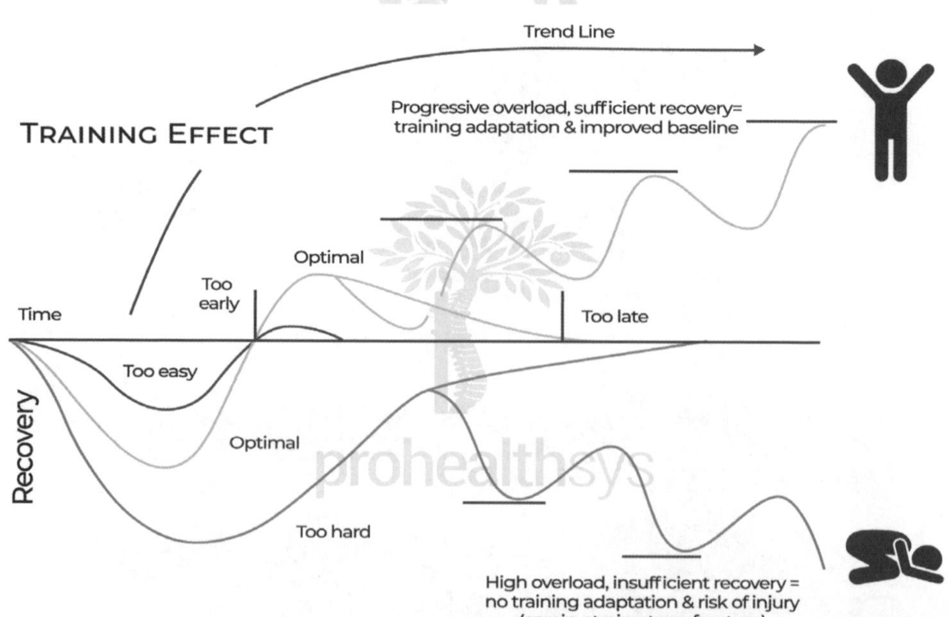

WHAT PEOPLE THINK LEADS TO PRODUCTIVITY

WHAT ACTUALLY DOES...

OPTIMAL PERFORMANCE

High
Performance (physical & mental)
Low
Sleep
Boredom
Interest
Excitement
Stress
Anxiety
Stress zone
Panic, choke
Low
Arousal Level
High

Based on the graph above, your goal is to work in the interest and excitement zones as much as possible, for all aspects of your life! Occasional stress is also needed for growth.

Lowering Stress

Diaphragmatic breathing[1]:

1. Sit or lay comfortably, eyes closed.
2. Relax your shoulders, let go of the tension in forehead, jaw, and eyes. Take your tongue of the roof of the mouth.
3. **Put a hand on your chest and a hand on your lower belly.**
4. Breathe in through your nose. Feel the air enter your nose, down your trachea, and entering your lungs. Feel your stomach rise to full expansion. Hold that breathe for 1-2 seconds.
5. Exhale through your mouth (pursed lips). Allow your stomach to depress (softly compress tummy if it helps).
6. Repeat these steps. Try to inhale and exhale for 4-8 seconds, holding for 1-2 seconds.

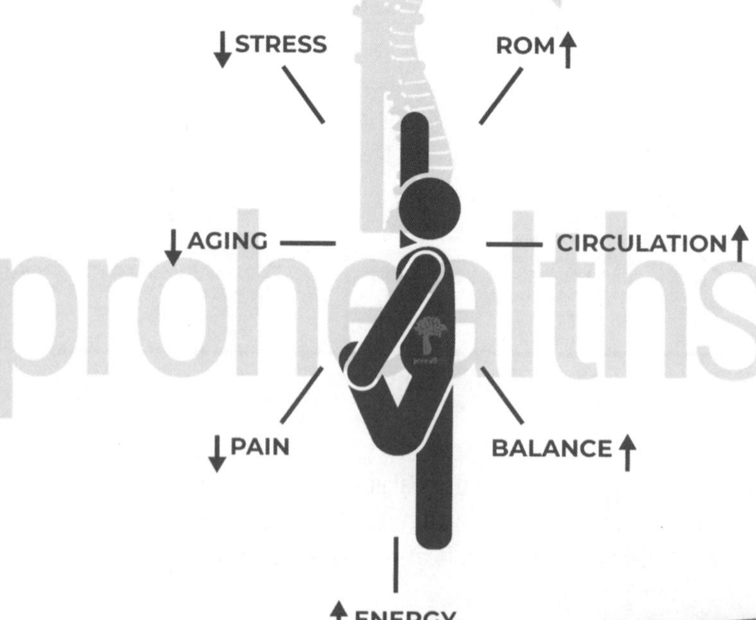

Lowering Stress

MEDICATION (with "T" correcting the "C": MEDITATION)

RELAXATION TECHNIQUES

6 EVIDENCE-BASED WAYS TO DE-STRESS MIND AND BODY

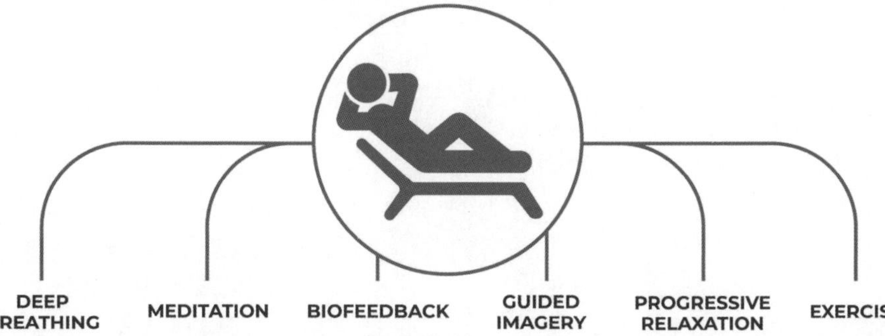

DEEP BREATHING

RELAXATION OF BODY AND MIND BY DEEP AND SLOW BREATHING

MEDITATION

MAINTAINING A MOMENT-BY-MOMENT AWARENESS OF THOUGHTS, FEELINGS AND BODILY SENSATIONS

BIOFEEDBACK

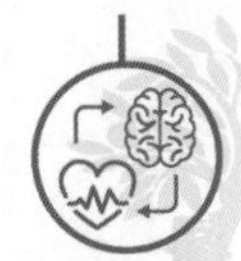

MONITORING OF A BODILY FUNCTION TO ACQUIRE VOLUNTARY CONTROL OF THIS FUNCTION

GUIDED IMAGERY

USE OF IMAGINATION TO PICTURE A SITUATION OR PLACE THAT MAKES YOU FEEL RELAXED

PROGRESSIVE RELAXATION

TENSING AND RELAXING OF MUSCLES TO INTENSIFY THE RELAXATION AFTER THE RELEASE

EXERCISE

EXERCISE AND OTHER FORMS OF BODYWORK CAN LEAD TO A STATE OF INCREASED RELAXATION

10 Day Fitness Diary (Diet & Exercise)

Day ___ Oatmeal & Blue Berries Coffee with doughnut Hamburger fries salad Bag of chips, pop Spaghetti, bread, caesar salad, 2 cups red wine morning stretch took stairs at work 10 min walk at break 2 circuits 'buns master' - was hard but felt good	Day ___
Day ___	Day ___
Day ___	Day ___
Day ___	Day ___
Day ___	Day ___

10 Day Fitness Diary (Diet & Exercise)

Day ___	Day ___
Day ___	Day ___
Day ___	Day ___
Day ___	Day ___
Day ___	Day ___

Exercise Performance Tracker

____
DATE

PREVIOUS BEST REPS:__________ WEIGHT:__________

SET 1 REPS:__________ (GOAL: 10-15) WEIGHT:__________

SET 2 REPS:__________ (GOAL: 8 -12) WEIGHT:__________

SET 3 REPS:__________ (GOAL: 6-8) WEIGHT:__________

SET 4 REPS:__________ (GOAL: 4-6) WEIGHT:__________

PREVIOUS BEST REPS:__________ WEIGHT:__________

SET 1 REPS:__________ (GOAL: 10-15) WEIGHT:__________

SET 2 REPS:__________ (GOAL: 8 -12) WEIGHT:__________

SET 3 REPS:__________ (GOAL: 6-8) WEIGHT:__________

SET 4 REPS:__________ (GOAL: 4-6) WEIGHT:__________

PREVIOUS BEST REPS:__________ WEIGHT:__________

SET 1 REPS:__________ (GOAL: 10-15) WEIGHT:__________

SET 2 REPS:__________ (GOAL: 8 -12) WEIGHT:__________

SET 3 REPS:__________ (GOAL: 6-8) WEIGHT:__________

SET 4 REPS:__________ (GOAL: 4-6) WEIGHT:__________

PREVIOUS BEST REPS:__________ WEIGHT:__________

SET 1 REPS:__________ (GOAL: 10-15) WEIGHT:__________

SET 2 REPS:__________ (GOAL: 8 -12) WEIGHT:__________

SET 3 REPS:__________ (GOAL: 6-8) WEIGHT:__________

SET 4 REPS:__________ (GOAL: 4-6) WEIGHT:__________

Weekly Progress Tracker

Goals:

WEEK 1 - Date: ____________

Weight: ________ Body Fat%: ________

Fat Weight: ________ Less Body Mass: ________

ADJUSTMENT TO MAKE

CALORIES ↑☐ ↓☐ —☐ ________

CARDIO ↑☐ ↓☐ —☐ ________

TRAINING INTENSITY ↑☐ ↓☐ —☐ ________

WEEK 2 - Date: ____________

Weight: ________ Body Fat%: ________

Fat Weight: ________ Less Body Mass: ________

ADJUSTMENT TO MAKE

CALORIES ↑☐ ↓☐ —☐ ________

CARDIO ↑☐ ↓☐ —☐ ________

TRAINING INTENSITY ↑☐ ↓☐ —☐ ________

WEEK 3 - Date: ____________

Weight: ________ Body Fat%: ________

Fat Weight: ________ Less Body Mass: ________

ADJUSTMENT TO MAKE

CALORIES ↑☐ ↓☐ —☐ ________

CARDIO ↑☐ ↓☐ —☐ ________

TRAINING INTENSITY ↑☐ ↓☐ —☐ ________

WEEK 4 - Date: ____________

Weight: ________ Body Fat%: ________

Fat Weight: ________ Less Body Mass: ________

ADJUSTMENT TO MAKE

CALORIES ↑☐ ↓☐ —☐ ________

CARDIO ↑☐ ↓☐ —☐ ________

TRAINING INTENSITY ↑☐ ↓☐ —☐ ________

WEEK 5 - Date: ____________

Weight: ________ Body Fat%: ________

Fat Weight: ________ Less Body Mass: ________

ADJUSTMENT TO MAKE

CALORIES ↑☐ ↓☐ —☐ ________

CARDIO ↑☐ ↓☐ —☐ ________

TRAINING INTENSITY ↑☐ ↓☐ —☐ ________

WEEK 6 - Date: ____________

Weight: ________ Body Fat%: ________

Fat Weight: ________ Less Body Mass: ________

ADJUSTMENT TO MAKE

CALORIES ↑☐ ↓☐ —☐ ________

CARDIO ↑☐ ↓☐ —☐ ________

TRAINING INTENSITY ↑☐ ↓☐ —☐ ________

Reps in a minute - how many body weight reps in 60 seconds?

Week	1	2	3	4	5	6
Sit-ups						
Push-ups						
J-Jacks						
Pull-ups						
Squats						
Burpee						
Plank time						

Get a base line of your ability

The following are **no-cost, fast, and simple measure that may be a useful and objective clinical assessment tool for evaluating functional capacity** and cardiovascular disease risk. See Exercise Therapy chapter for more details.

Push Ups (straight reps, no rest)

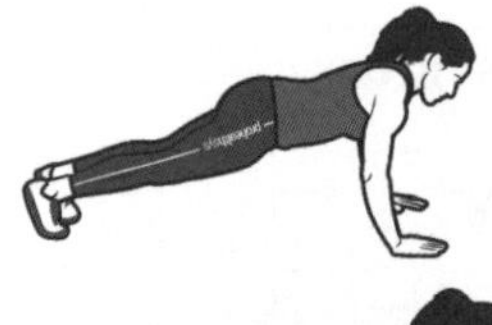

	Poor	Novice	Mid.	Advance	Elite	WR
Women	< 1	6	20	37	56	10,507
Men	3	19	42	70	100	

Study of 1104 occupationally active adult men found a significant negative association between baseline push-up capacity and incident cardiovascular disease risk across 10 years of follow-up. Participants able to complete more than 40 push-ups were associated with a significant reduction in incident cardiovascular disease event risk compared with those completing fewer than 10 push-ups. Yang J, Christophi CA, Farioli A, et al. Association Between Push-up Exercise Capacity and Future Cardiovascular Events Among Active Adult Men. JAMA Netw Open. 2019;2(2):e188341. doi:10.1001/jamanetworkopen.2018.8341 WR = Wold record: 10,507 by Minoru Yoshida (Japan)

Pull-ups (reps in 1 minute)

	Poor	Novice	Mid	Advance	Elite
Women	< 1	1	5	15	25
Men	<1	5	14	25	35

WR = wold record: 68 Adam Sandel (USA)

Plank Test (hold time in seconds, on elbows or hands)

	Poor	Novice	Mid	Advance	Elite	WR
Women	20	50	100	150	230	4⁺ hr
Men	35	70	110	165	240	8⁺ hr

WR = wold record. Female: Dana Glowacka (Canada) 4 hours, 20 min. Male: Mao Weidong (China) 8 hr 1 min.

Single leg balance time (eyes closed)

Age	18-39	40-49	50-59	60-69	70+
Women/men	8.5 sec	7.4	5.2	2.5	2.0

Better balance is associated with decreased risk of fall related injuries, as age progresses. Consider encouraging patients to stand on one leg when brushing teeth or working at a counter to improve ability.

Sit and Reach Test

The ACSM and the Canadian Society for Exercise Physiology recommend the standard sit-and-reach test to assess hip and hamstring flexibility. Client sits on the floor with their knees extended and the soles of their feet against the box with heels 15 cm (6") apart. Keeping their knees and arms straight, client reaches forward, palms down, as far as they can and hold position for 2 seconds. Record the farthest distance. Repeat 3 times and record maximum number.

Ranks for Modified Sit-and-Reach Test*

age	≤35 yr	36-49 yr	≥50 yr
Excellent	≥17.9 cm	≥17.4	≥15.0
Very Good	16.2-16.7	15.2-16.2	13.6-14.2
Good	14.8-15.8	13.5-14.5	11.1-12.3
Fair	13.7-14.5	12.2-12.8	9.2-10.1
Low	≤12.6	≤11.0	≤8.3

*Sit-and-reach scores measured to the nearest 0.25 in.(0.6 cm). From W.W.K. Hoeger, 1999, Lifetime physical fitness & wellness (Englewood, CO: Morton Publishing Co.).

Get a base line of your ability

Squat Body Weight (reps, no rest thighs to horizontal)

	Poor	Novice	Mid	Advance	Elite
Women	< 1	12	39	74	113
Men	1	22	53	91	133

Squat and Rise Test

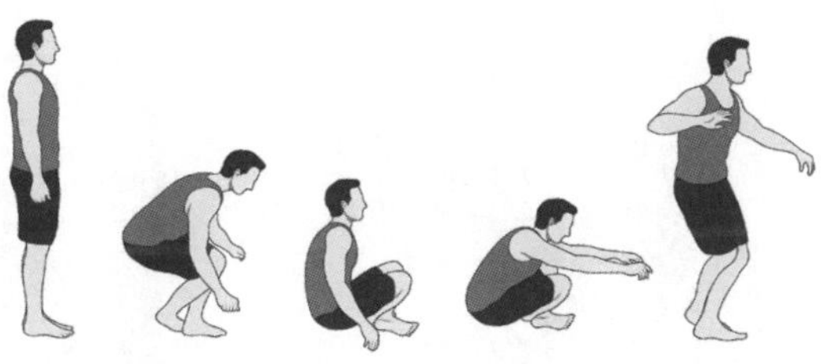

The **ability to squat and rise in patients has been correlated with life expectancy** - test is scored between 1 and 10 (5 points for sitting, 5 more points for standing back up). Each time you use an arm or knee for help in balancing during the test, you subtract one point from 10 possible points. Half a point is subtracted each time you lose balance, or when the fluidity of the feat becomes clumsy. Patients aged 51 to 80, and found that people who scored less than 8 points on the test were twice as likely to die within the next six years (sample size was 2000+ people)

- Brito, LB, et. al. Ability to sit and rise from the floor as a predictor of all-cause mortality - European Journal of Preventive Cardiology 2047487312471759, December 13, 2012

Minus 1 point each if...

Reps in a minute - how many body weight reps in 60 seconds?

	Poor	Novice	Mid	Advance	Elite	WR
Sit-ups	1-5	6-15	16-25	26-39	40+	82
Push-ups	< 5	5-15	16-25	29-39	40+	140
J-Jacks	1-25	26-35	40-49	50-59	60+	116
Pull-ups	< 1	1-5	6-14	15-26	26+	68
Squats	< 10	10-15	16-25	26-35	36+	70
Burpee	< 1	1-5	6-14	14-20	21+	47

1 & 1 FUN

1 min per exercise | **1 min** rest

(level 1 = 1 circuit, 2 = 3 circuits, 40 sec rest, 3 = 5 circuits, 30 sec rest)

Welcome to interval training. Time on, time off with a focus on cardiovascular fitness and burning fat. It is fun!

Squat

Jumping Jacks

Side Leg Raises

Lunges Step-Ups

Diagonal Plank

Mountain Climber

Swimmer

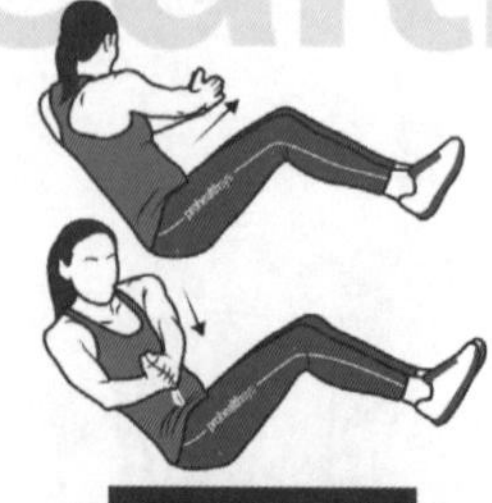

Russian Twist

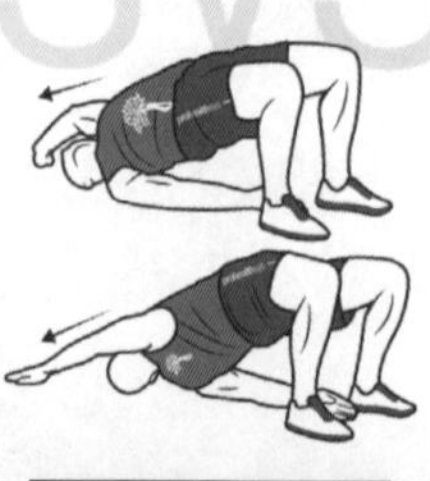

Bridge and Reach

2 Minute Joy

20 sec per exercise | no rest

(level 1 = 2 cycles, 2 = 4 cycles, 3 = 5 cycles)

Find joy with this lower body explosive power routine.

Step-Up

Tuck Jumps

Side Lunge

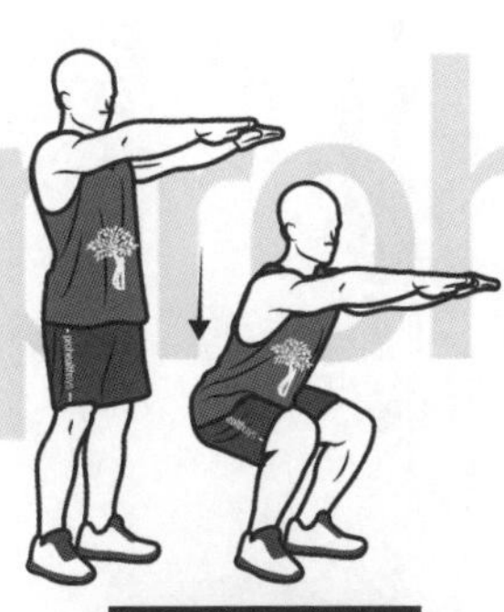

Squat

Plank Jump-Ins

Leg Plank

3+ Burpee

10 sec per exercise | no rest

(level 1 = 2 cycles, 2 = 4 cycles, 3 = 5 cycles)

Welcome to the wonderful world of burpees! You'll count your lucky stars when this SUPERSET session is done.

High Knees

Mountain Climber

Shoulder Taps

Burpee

4 Door

10 sec per exercise | no rest

(level 1 = 1 cycles, 2 = 3 cycles, 3 = 5 cycles)

You have 4 limbs and all can be used to open doors.
Enjoy this appendage focus parade of power.

5 Alive

10 of each exercise | rest after circuit

(level 1 = 2 cycles, 2 = 4 cycles, 3 = 6 cycles)

There is good research to support 5x5 workout, but be warned this is a more challenging session...

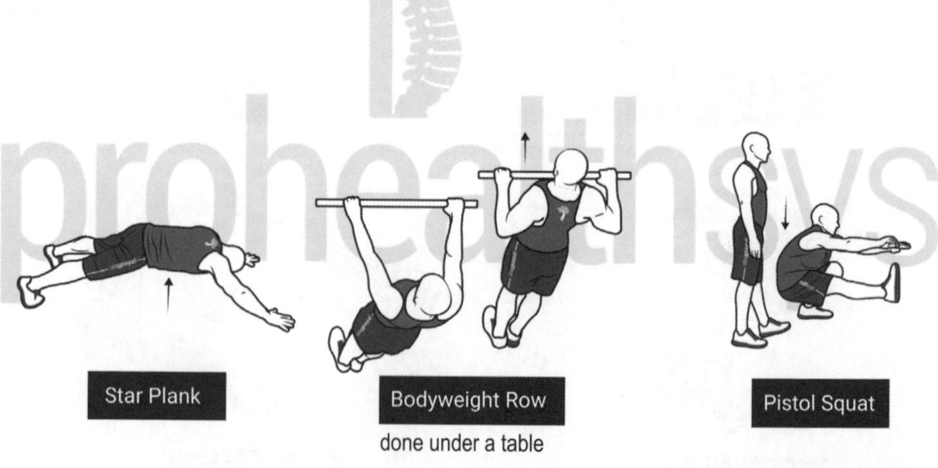

6 in Sticks

20 sec per exercise | no rest

(level 1 = 2 cycles, 2 = 4 cycles, 3 = 6 cycles with a sledge hammer)

Get that broom out of the closet and clean up your body. Dowels, shovels or sledge hammers work too - either way swing a stick and feel slick!

Swimmer

Infinity spins

Standing half lotus

Dead lift jump

Overhead squat

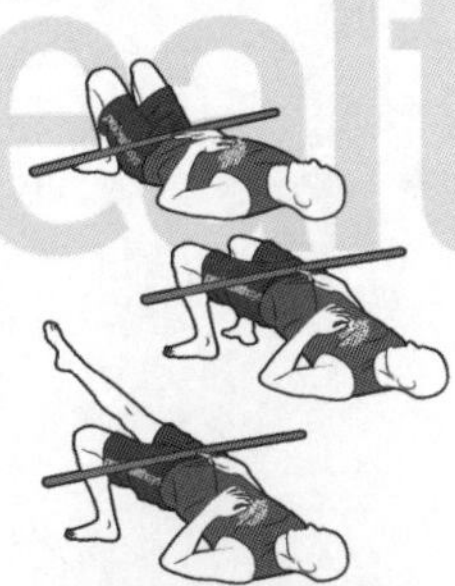

Single leg raise

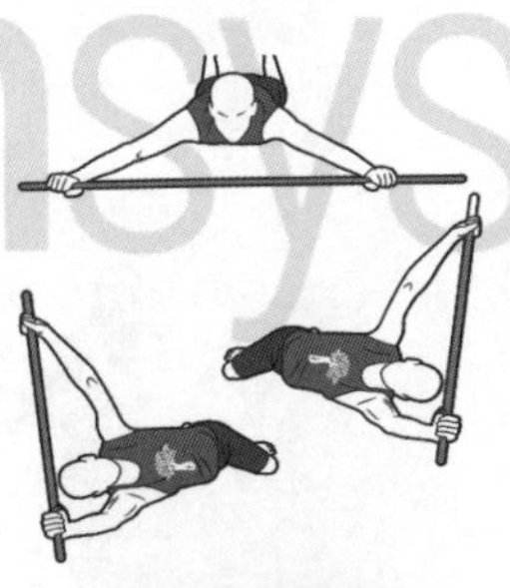

Lying twist

7th Heaven

10 sec per exercise | no rest

(level 1 = 2 cycles, 2 = 4 cycles, 3 = 6 cycles)

Here is a lower body blast to improve leg power and firm the thighs and gluteals. Every step just a little closer to heaven!

High Knees

Lunge

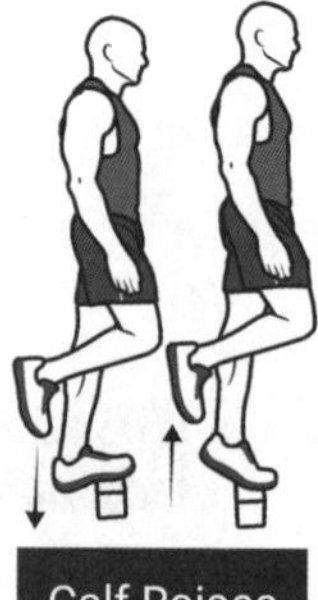

Calf Raises

Get-Ups

Single Leg Dead Lift

Turning Kicks

Sumo Squat

Gr8 Date

10 of each exercise | rest after circuit

(level 1 = 2 cycles, 2 = 4 cycles, 3 = 6 cycles)

Today is a great date to complete this fun circuit. Work your chest and back while your frustrations melt away.

9 yard line

10 sec per exercise | rest after circuit

(level 1 = 2 cycles, 2 = 4 cycles, 3 = 6 cycles)

This foot ball inspired game will improve lower body power and jump height. Get ready for take off!

High Knees

Lunges Step-Ups

Sumo Squat

Side Skater Jump

Box Jumps

Step-Up

10-10

10 of each exercise | rest after circuit

(level 1 = 2x, level 2 = 5x, level 3 = 10x)

10 seconds of 10 exercises will help make you body and lungs a perfect 10!

Split Squat

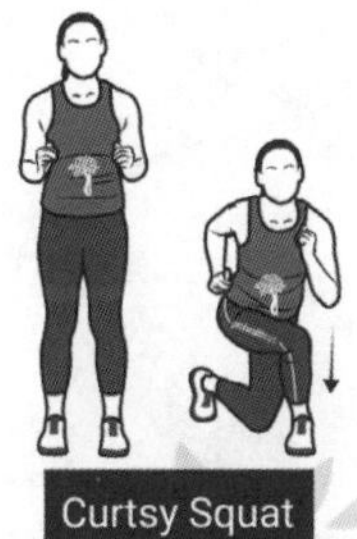

Curtsy Squat

Plank Rotations

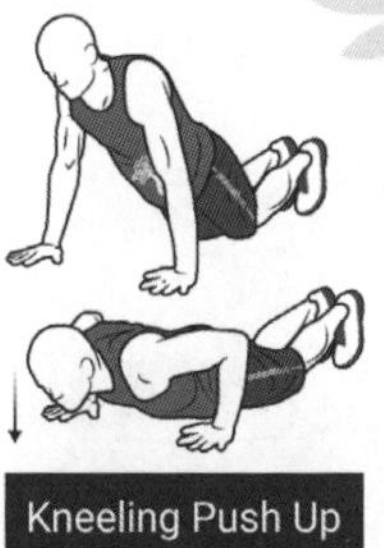

Kneeling Push Up

T-Spine Rotation

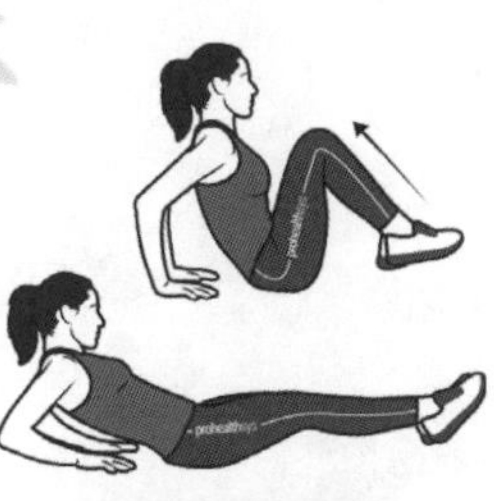

Leg Pull-In

Bridge and Reach

Oblique Crunch

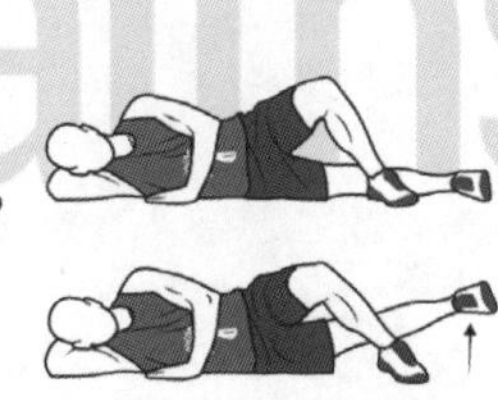

Adductor Leg Raise

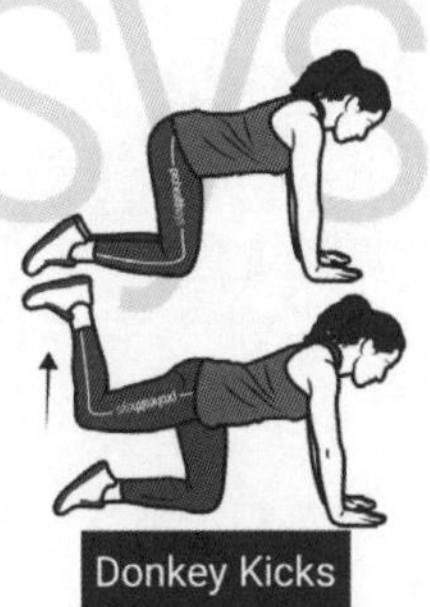

Donkey Kicks

Abs of Steel

10 of each exercise | rest after circuit

(level 1 = 2 cycles, 2 = 4 cycles, 3 = 6 cycles)

While we know abs are made in the kitchen, good core stability can help you in every aspect of life. Improve your posture enjoy this ab-blaster!

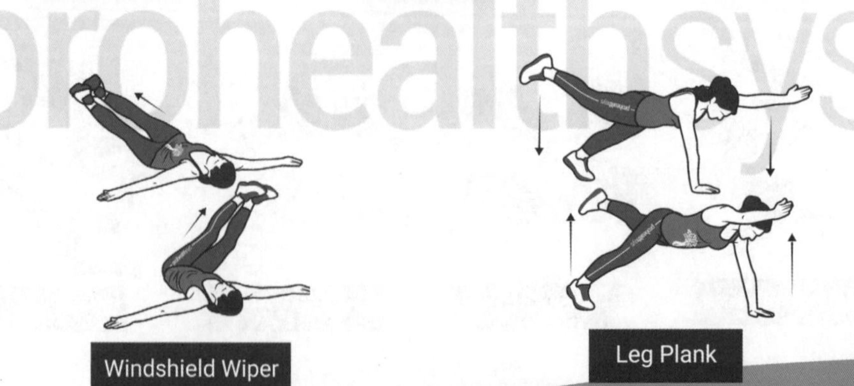

Acorn

20 sec per exercise | rest after circuit

(level 1 = 2x, level 2 = 4x, level 3 = 6x)

Like the mighty oak, we start as a seed that grows based
on the stresses survived in life. Grow Tall!

Upward Salute

Warrior II

Goddess Squat

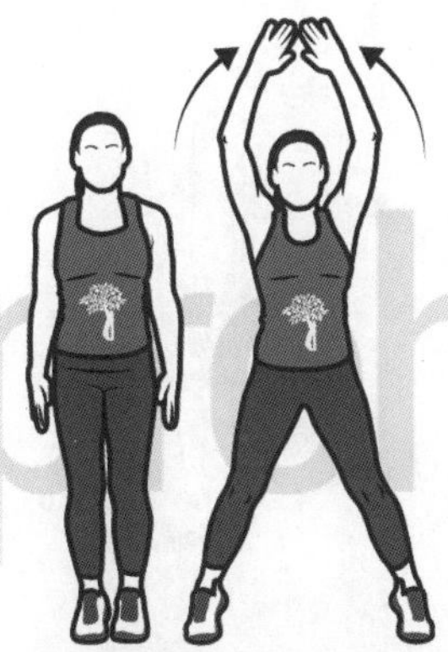

Jumping Jacks

Warrior I

Tree Pose

Ankle Fix

30 secs ON | 20 secs rest after each exercise

(level 1 = 2x, level 2 = 4x, level 3 = 6x)

If you have ankle sprains this is for you. Sprains damage ligaments, muscles and nerves. Moving in **relatively pain free actions** can speed recovery and prevent future injury

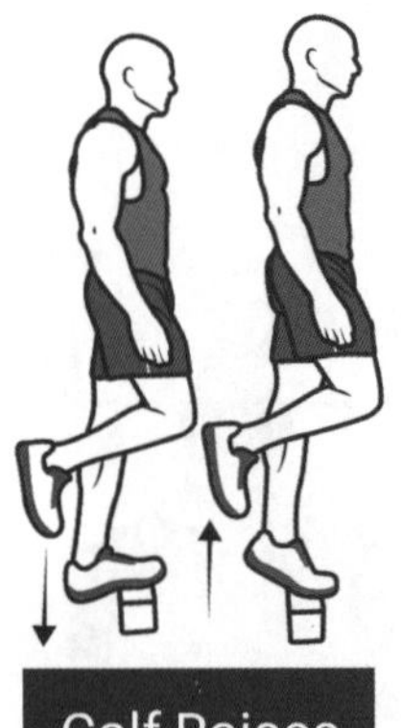

Calf Raises

Walking Toe Touches

Side Leg Raises

Calf Extension

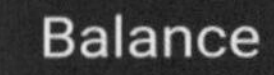

Balance

Sole rolls

Bacon

40 secs ON | 20 secs rest after each exercise

(level 1 = 2x, level 2 = 5x, level 3 = 10x)

Bring home the bacon! This heart pumping 'belly burning' cardio routine is sure to make you hungry.

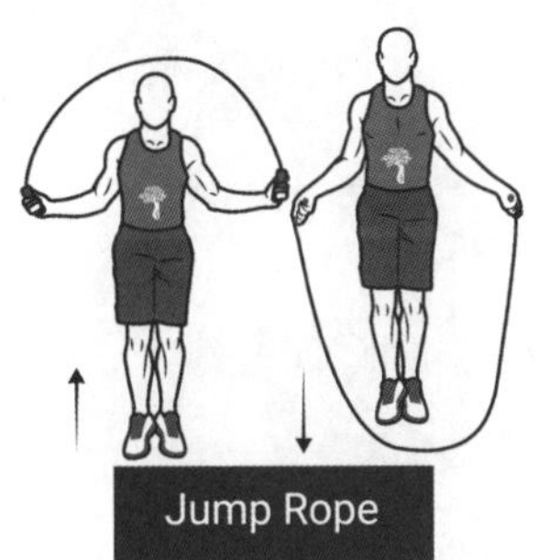

Jump Rope

Plank Jump-Ins

Crab Walk

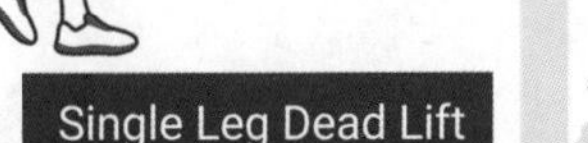

Single Leg Dead Lift

Bird Dog

Pseudo Planche

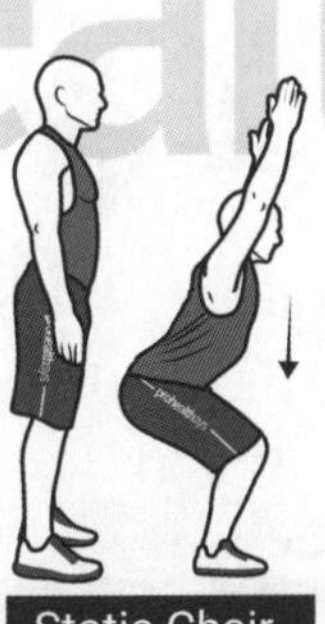

Static Chair Pose

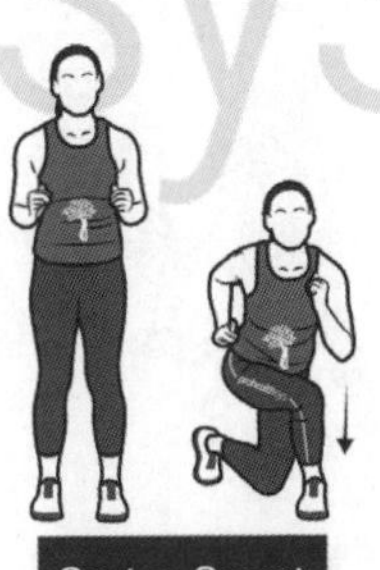

Curtsy Squat

Buns Master

10 of each exercise | rest after circuit

(level 1 = 2x, level 2 = 5x, level 3 = 10x)

This great butt burner will be sure to add more junk in your trunk... in a good way #bubblebutt ☺

Tuck Jumps

Step-Up

Donkey Kicks

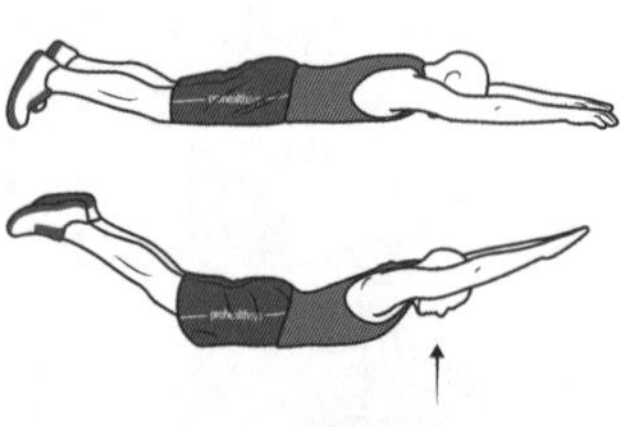

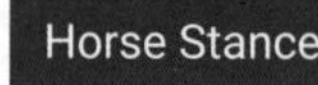

Superman

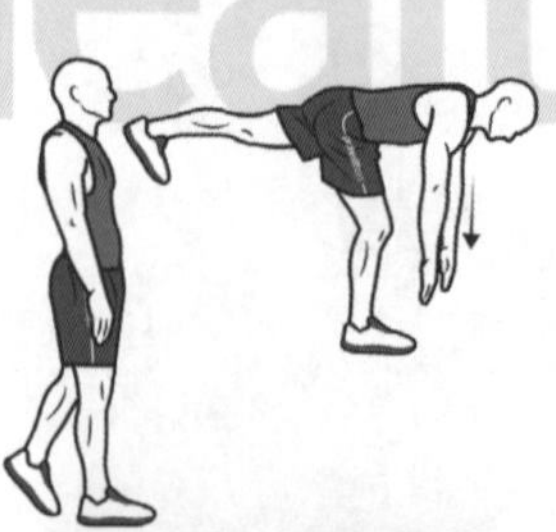

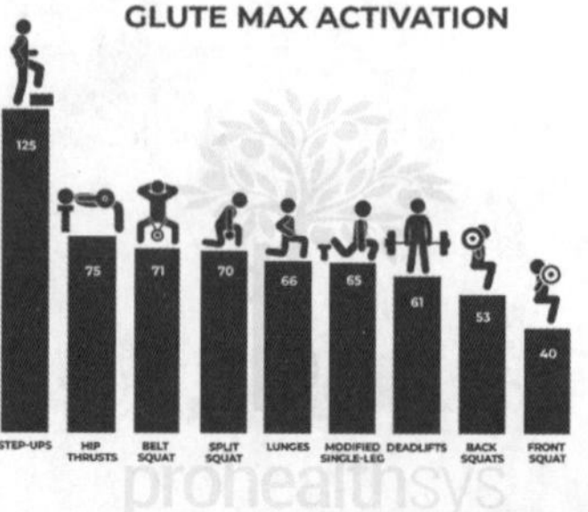

Sumo Squat

Single Leg Dead Lift

BBQ

10 of each exercise | rest after circuit

(level 1 = 2x, level 2 = 5x, level 3 = 10x)

Hungry for some gains? Get ready to salivate over developing your own sweet tenderloin and rump-roast with the bbq... it's hot.

YTWL

Jump Rope

Side Lying Leg Lift

Donkey Kicks

Bird Dog

Mountain Climber

Full Arch

Side Lunge

Split Squat

Big Boy

2 minutes rest after each set

(level 1 = 3x, level 2 = 5x, level 3 = 7x)

Who wants to be a big boy? Try this fun routine to help you grow up big and strong.

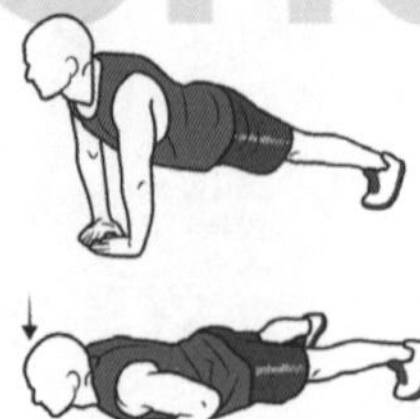

50 high knees

5 push-ups

50 high knees

5 burpees

50 high knees

5 closed grip push ups

Bod Mod

Rest after each exercise 60 sec max

(level 1 = 2x, level 2 = 5x, level 3 = 8x)

Welcome to the world of pyramid training. Climb to the apex of the mountain and back down for a true sense of accomplishment

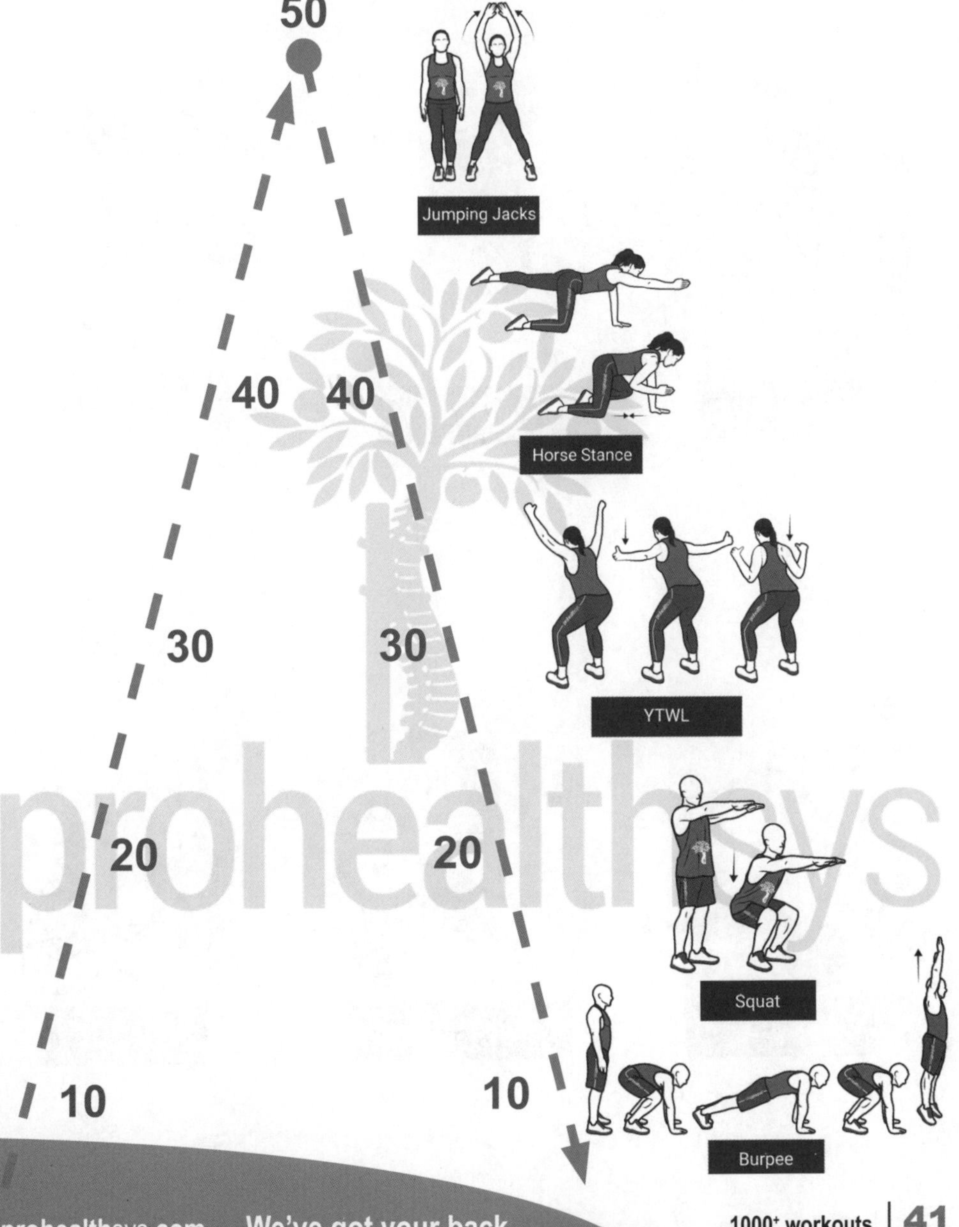

Cardio Demon

40 secs ON | 20 secs rest after each exercise

(level 1 = 2x, level 2 = 5x, level 3 = 10x)

Develop the cardiovascular capacity to out run the demons of your life with this hear pumping extravaganza.

Combat Kid

10 of each exercise | rest after circuit

(level 1 = 2x, level 2 = 5x, level 3 = 10x)

Get ready for your next fight. With these proven power moves, you'll be unstoppable!

X Factor

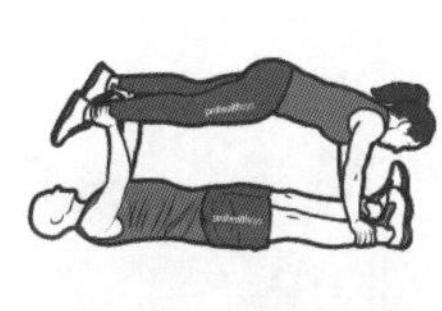

Sync PushUps

Oil Drill

Better Back

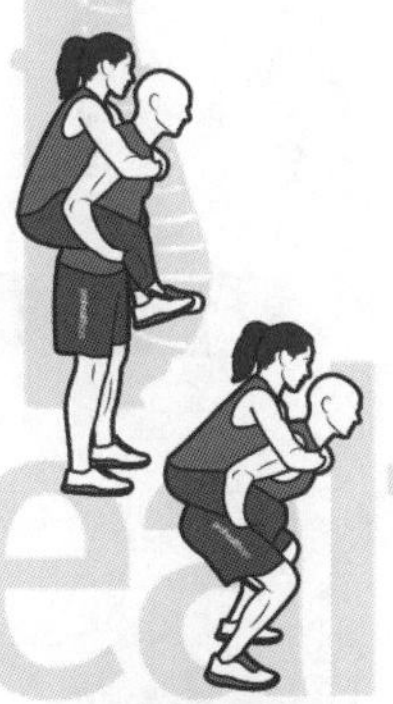

Carry me

Bicycle

Centurion

40 secs ON | 20 secs rest after each exercise

(level 1 = 2x, level 2 = 5x, level 3 = 10x)

Like the names sake, use these to develope your leadership as a professional officer in the Roman army.

External wrist twist

Inchworm

High Knees

Close Grip Push-Ups

YTWL

Rack Push Press

Rack Squat

Sumo Squat

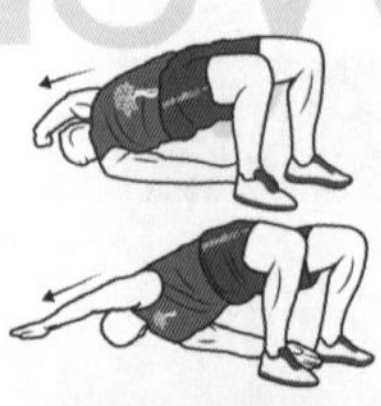

Bridge and Reach

Commando

10 of each exercise | rest after circuit

(level 1 = 2x, level 2 = 5x, level 3 = 10x)

Go commando, and look better naked with this toning firming routine you are sure to get hard.

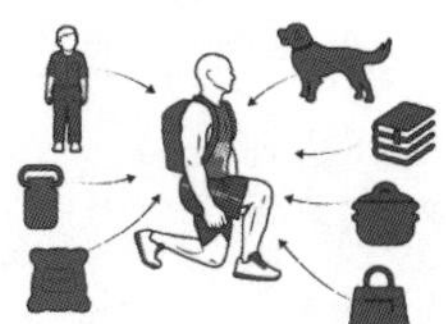

Damage Control

rest after each cycle

(level 1 = 2x, level 2 = 5x, level 3 = 10x)

Develop the resilience you need to avoid injury and damage to your body with this sweet routine.

50 high knees

5 push-ups

40 jumping jacks

5 plank jumps

50 high knees

10 leg pull ins

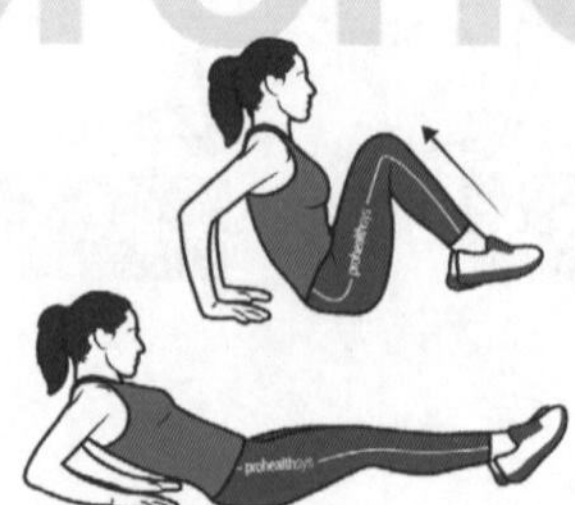

Dead Pool

10 of each exercise | rest after circuit

(level 1 = 2x, level 2 = 5x, level 3 = 10x)

Get your mojo back and postpone death with every rep in the killer circuit.

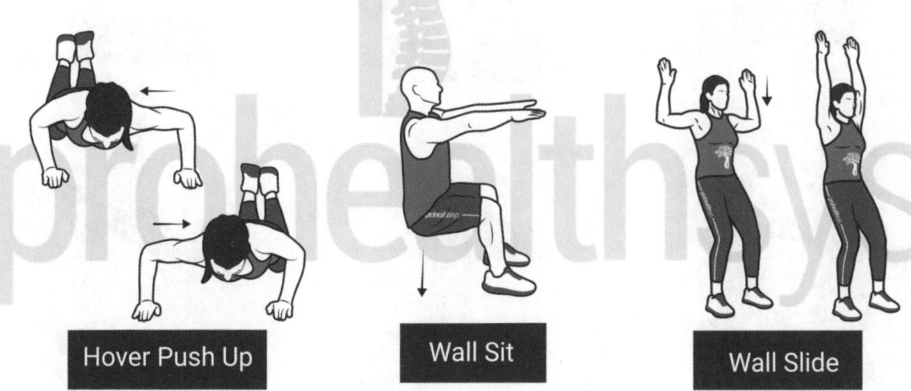

Dirty 30^{x3}

8-12 of each exercise | **rest** after circuit

(level 1 = 3x, level 2 = 6x, level 3 = 10x)

The dirty thirty x 3 will have you sweat, wet and looking forward to hitting the showers in a good way! The fast slow reps help train different muscle fibers.

Squat

fast

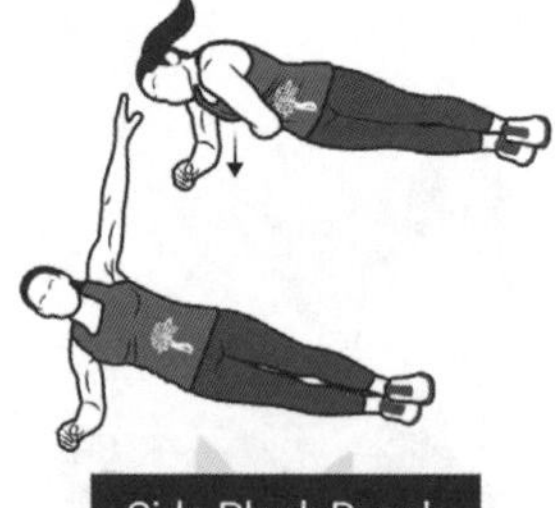

Side Plank Reach

Squat

slow

Step-Up

fast

Shoulder Taps

Step-Up

slow

Push-Up

fast

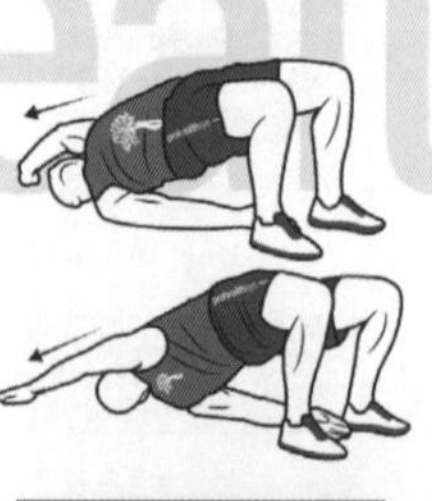

Bridge and Reach

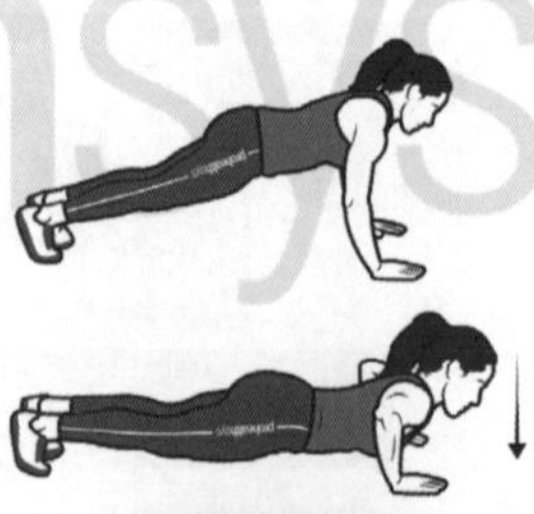

Push-Up

slow

Ender Bender

30 sec hold of each side

(level 1 = 2x, level 2 = 5x, level 3 = 10x)

This flexibility based routine is sure to improve your range of motion and pliability with fun!

Goddess Squat

Warrior II

Extended Triangle

Seated Twist

Pigeon

Down Dog

Plow

Garland

Happy Baby

Express-O

Rest after each exercise

(level 1 = 2x, level 2 = 5x, level 3 = 10x)

Hard to start your day without a cup of Joe? This caffeinic cycle will put the pep back in your step.

Extra Spice

12 of each exercise | rest after circuit

(level 1 = 2x, level 2 = 5x, level 3 = 10x)

Variety is the spice of life, grab soup cans, pots or milk jugs and turn up your life with a little extra spice... it sure will be nice!

Wood Chop

Lunge and Rotation

Single Leg Scarecrow

Alt.Shoulder Press

V-Sit Cross Jab

Single Leg Dead Lift

Stance Switch Swing

Goblet Squat

Renegade Row

Feelin Fine

40 secs ON | 20 secs rest after each exercise

(level 1 = 2x, level 2 = 5x, level 3 = 10x)

Grab a kettle bell (or bag, pot, pail or even small kids). With your spine in line, you're 'feelin fine.' This core based routine will help improve your spinal stabilization an lower the risk of back pain.

Good Morning

Thruster

Clean and Jerk

Dead Lift

Figure Eight

Side Plank

Turkish Get-Ups

Femme Fatale

10 of each exercise | rest after circuit

(level 1 = 2x, level 2 = 5x, level 3 = 10x)

Become a female assassin with a rock hard body and sharp mind to match... you are the femme fatale.

Step-Up

Box Jumps

Plank Rotations

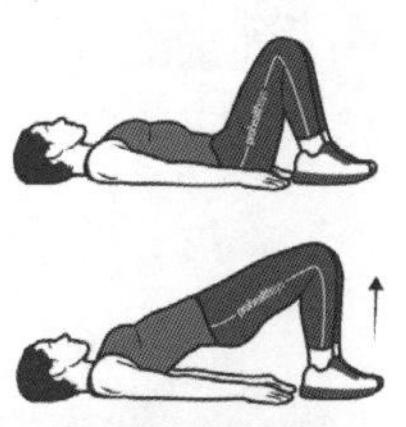

Hip Raise

Sumo Squat

Pike Push-Up

YTWL

Punches

Fighter

40 secs ON | 20 secs rest after each exercise

(level 1 = 2x, level 2 = 4x, level 3 = 6x)

Develop you killer moves with these basic combat drill to improve speed, strength and power. Be the fighter!

Get Flying

Varies based on skill

(level 1 = 2x, level 2 = 5x, level 3 = 8x)

Test your skill, strength and balance with this partner oriented acrobatic experiment #partnerflying.

Gladiator

rest after circuit

(level 1 = 2x, level 2 = 5x, level 3 = 10x)

Prepare for battle in the coliseum. Move your way to victory and personal gains for the glory of all. (also play the gladiator soundtrack in the background during this routine)

50 jumping jacks

10 plank rotations

40 step-ups

10 y-t-w

30 high knees

10 boat twists

Gravity 9.8

12 reps, 3 secs up 3, secs down each exercise

(level 1 = 2x, level 2 = 5x, level 3 = 8x)

Gravity is your friend, and slow is control. For this eccentric inspired program focus on fighting gravity and slowly letting your body drop... take the negatives for a positive outcome!

Step-Up

Overhead squat

Bodyweight Row

Leg Pull-In

Close Grip Push-Ups

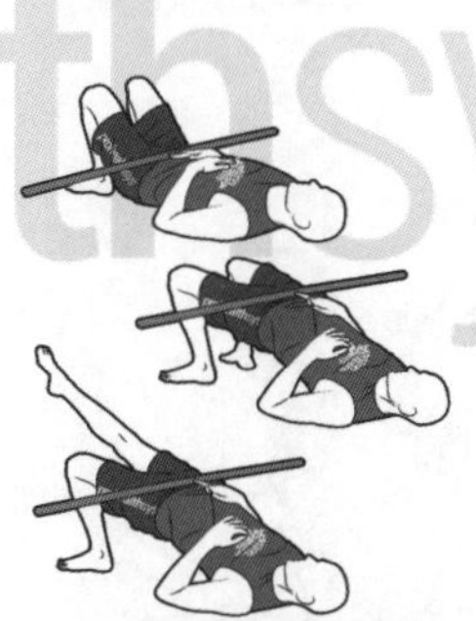

Single leg raise

Heat Pump

40 secs ON | 20 secs rest after each exercise

(level 1 = 2x, level 2 = 5x, level 3 = 10x)

Turn the temperature up and work in a hot environment to get your sweat on... a body cleansing experience!

Deadlift

Roll Out

Overhead Squat

Landmine Overhead Press

Hang Clean and Press

Glute Hamstring Raise

Hells Bells

5, 10, 15 of each exercise | rest after circuit

(level 1 = 3x, level 2 = 10x, level 3 = 20x)

This is an amazing gain builder, the goal is
100 pull-ups, 200 push-ups and 300 squats.

5 pull-ups

10 push-ups

15 squats

Hero

40 secs ON | 20 secs rest after each exercise

(level 1 = 2x, level 2 = 4x, level 3 = 6x)

Be a hero, save your body from a slow decay with this fun and elastic circuit. #elasticfantastic

Thruster

Wood Chop

Bent-over Side Raise

Alternating Row

Lateral Band Walk

Side Plank Row

Single-Leg Glute Bridge

Preacher Curls

Hercules

8-12 of each exercise | rest after each

(level 1 = 2x, level 2 = 3x, level 3 = 5x)

Learn some basic olympic lift movement patterns to develop the body of a greek god.
Start with just a broom or staff to move safely and gradually increase your weight.

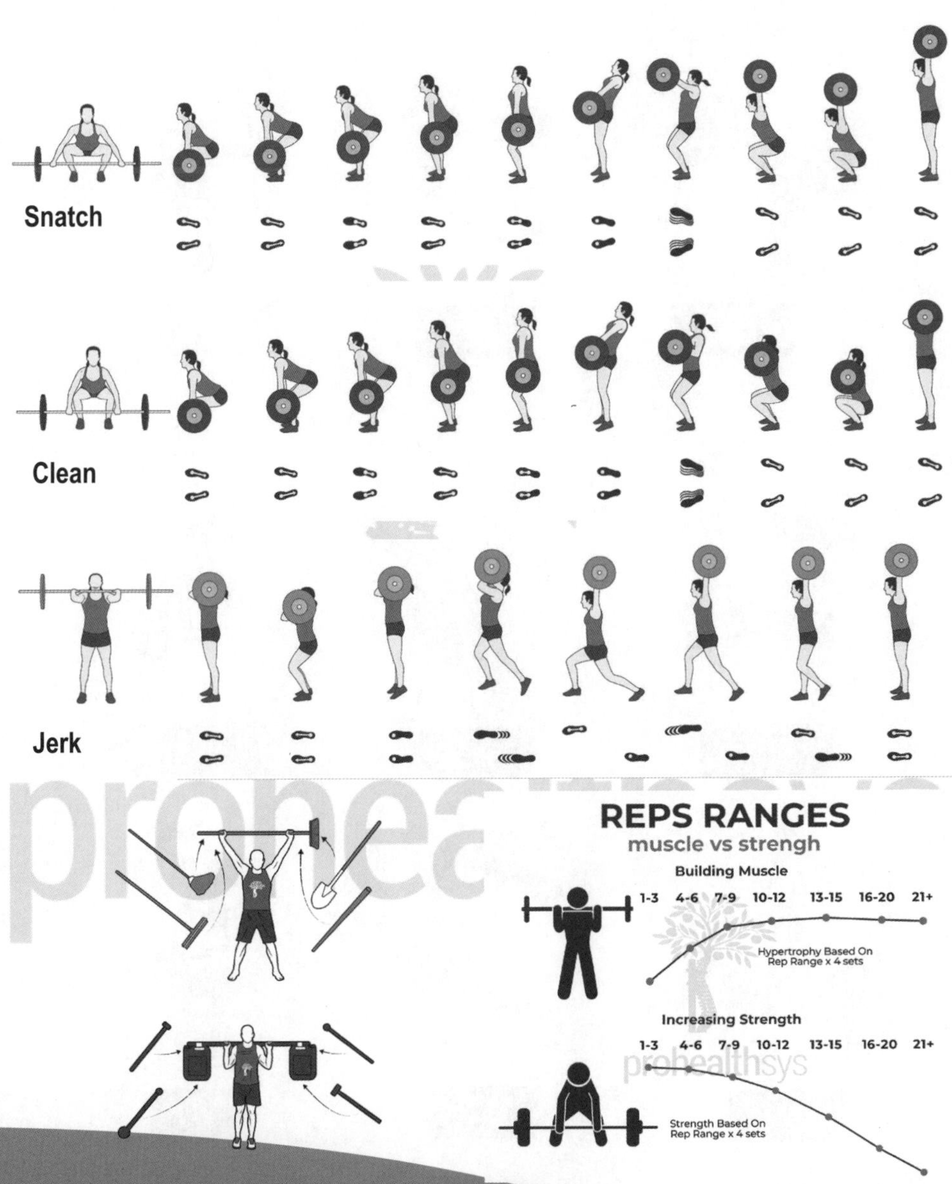

Iron Maiden

40 secs ON | 20 secs rest after each exercise

(level 1 = 2x, level 2 = 4x, level 3 = 6x)

Rock-on with this heavy metal routine. Turn up your tunes and start blasting away.

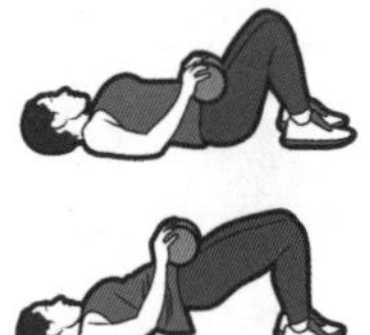

Single Arm Swing

Glute Bridge

Squat Hammer Curl

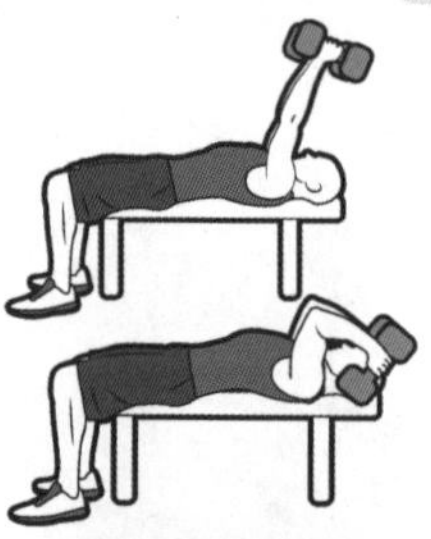

Skull Crusher

Side Swing

Weighted Lunge

180 Swing

Side Plank Row

Bent-Over-Row

Infinity ∞

15-20 reps each exercise | rest after circuit

(level 1 = 2x, level 2 = 5x, level 3 = 10x)

This endurance based circuit will help give you never ending stamina to accomplish your life goals.

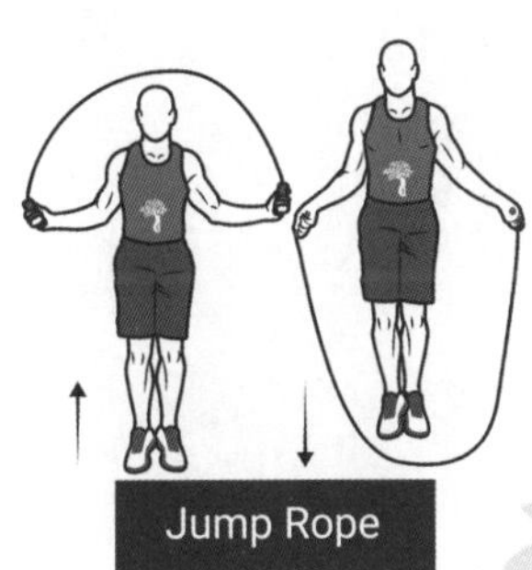

Jump Rope

Step-Up

Plank Jump-Ins

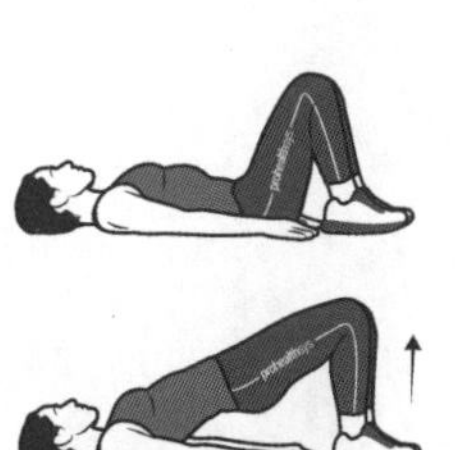

Hip Raise

Horse Stance

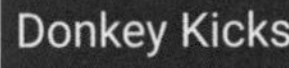

Donkey Kicks

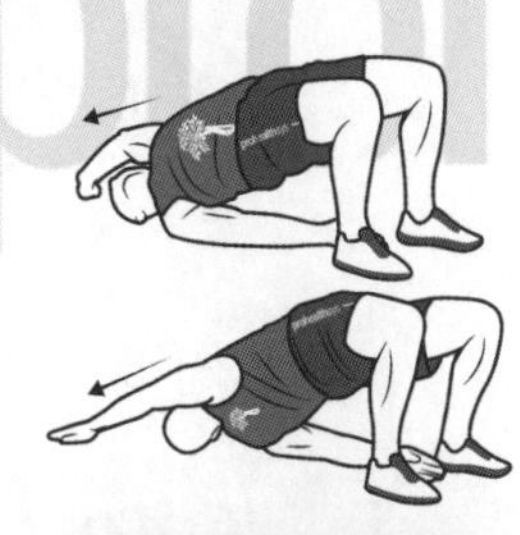

Bridge and Reach

Plank Rotations

ENDURANCE
(1-2 sets, 15+ reps)

Jack & Jill

rest after each exercise

(level 1 = 2x, level 2 = 4x, level 3 = 6x)

Jack and Jill went up the hill to fetch a pail of water...
Jack fell down and Jill came tumbling after

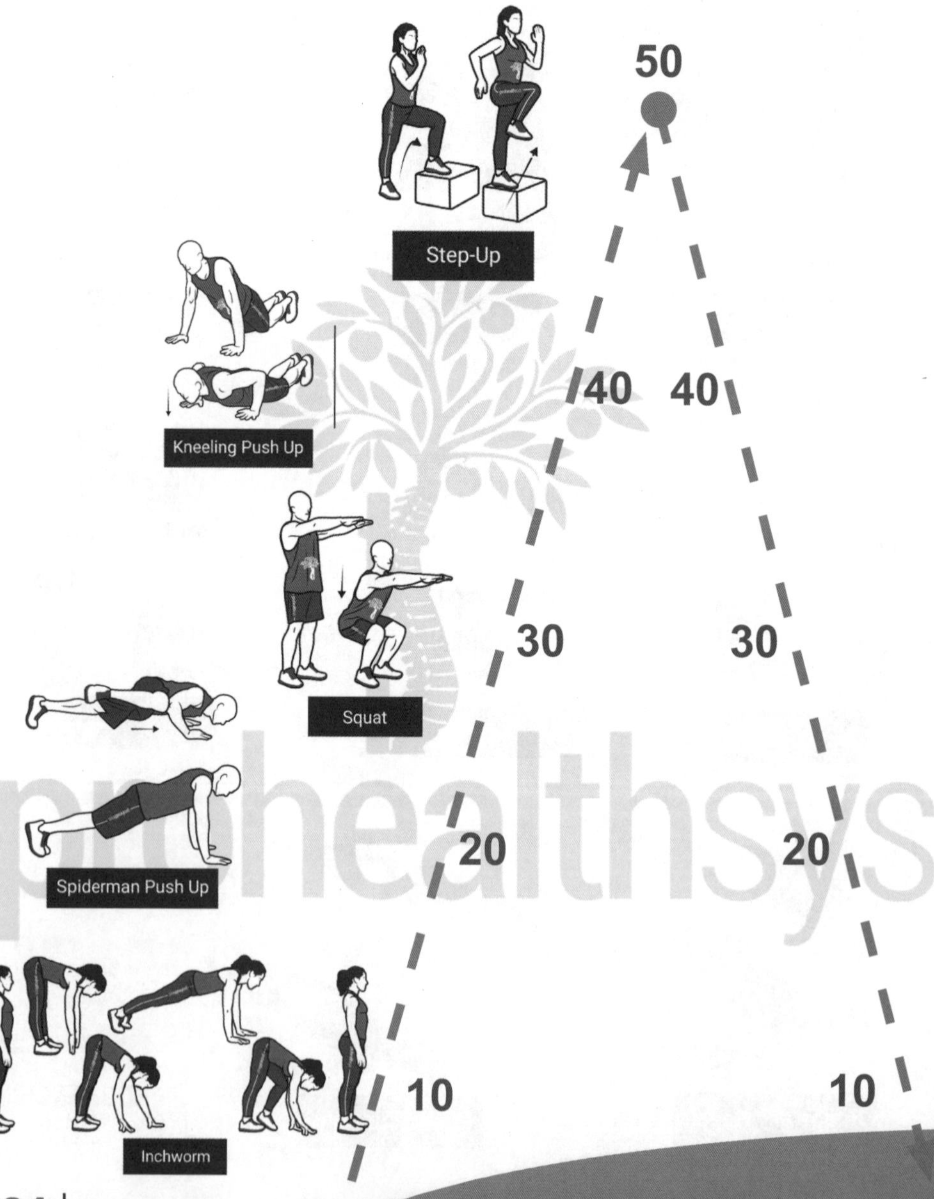

Leg Day

10 of each exercise | rest after circuit

(level 1 = 2x, level 2 = 5x, level 3 = 10x)

Do you like Jello? This sweet session will make your legs feel weak, and come back stronger than ever!

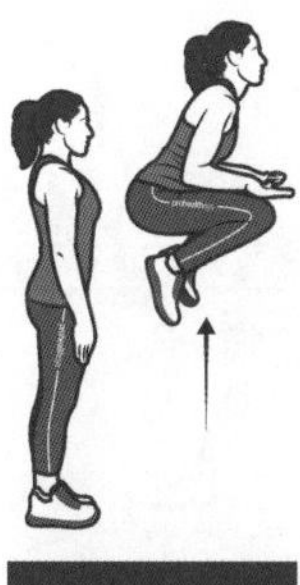

Tuck Jumps

Step-Up

Squat

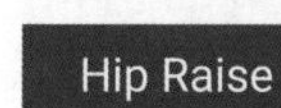

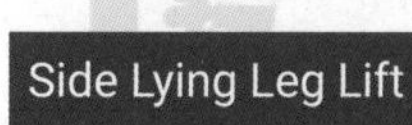

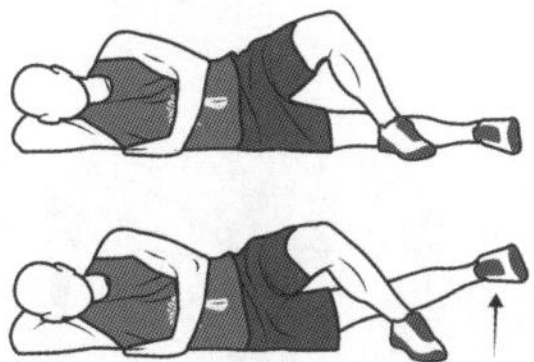

Adductor Leg Raise

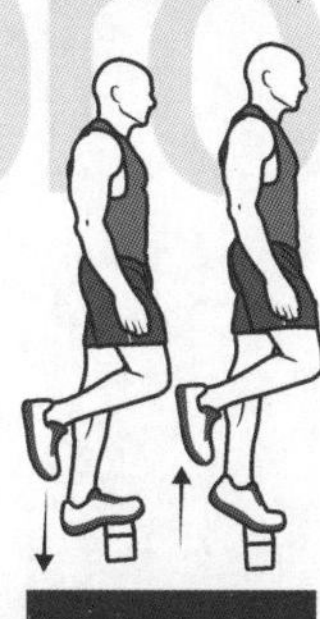

Calf Raises

Sumo Squat

Single Leg Dead Lift

Live Long

40 secs ON | 20 secs rest after each exercise

(level 1 = 2x, level 2 = 5x, level 3 = 10x)

Exercise improves both the quantity and quality of your life. Live long and prosper!

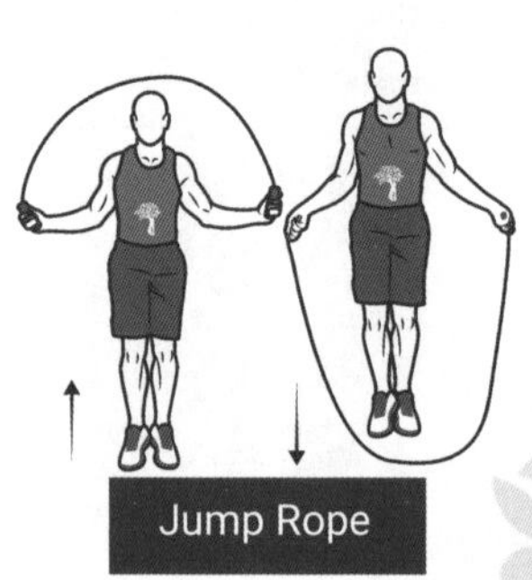

Jump Rope

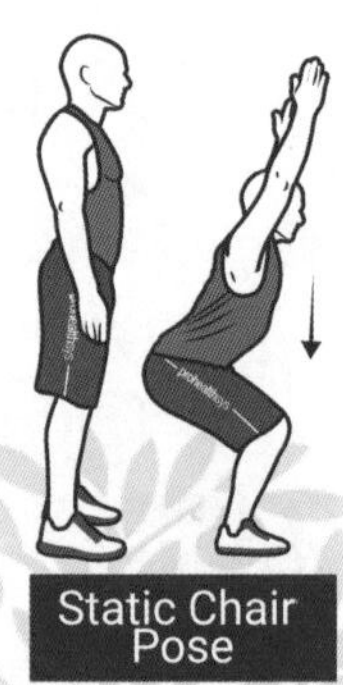

Static Chair Pose

Sumo Squat

YTWL

Bird Dog

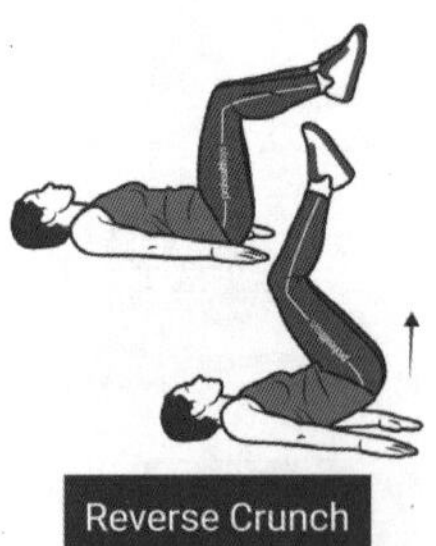

Reverse Crunch

Kneeling Push Up

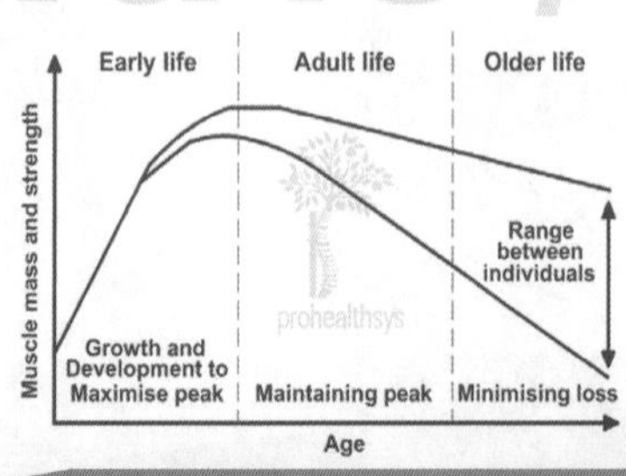

Lower Back

8-12 of each exercise | rest after circuit

(level 1 = 2x, level 2 = 5x, level 3 = 10x)

Low back pain is common, help fight back with this back strengthening circuit with exercises used by rehab specialist around the world

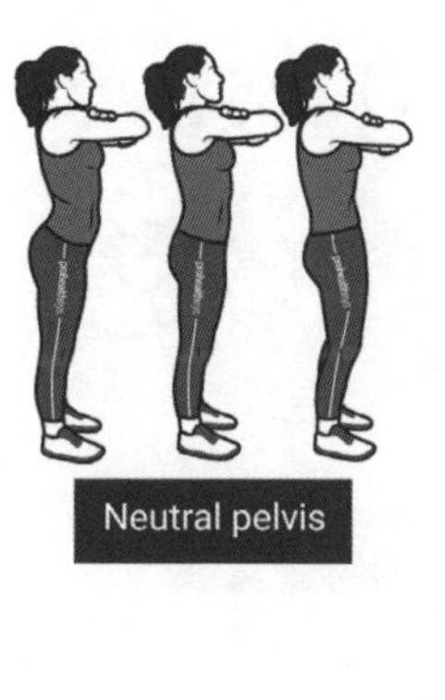

Neutral pelvis

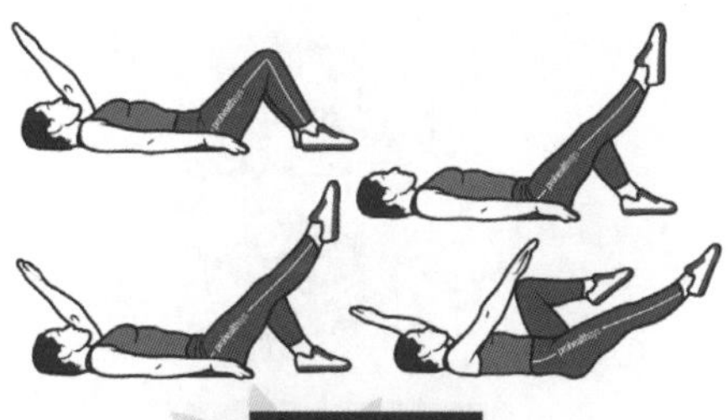

Dead Bug

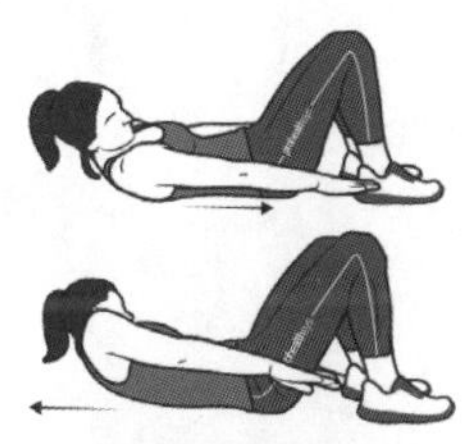

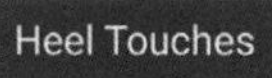

Heel Touches

Cobra

Diagonal Plank

Bird Dog

Squat

Walking Toe Touches

Bridge and Reach

No Surrender

20 secs ON | 20 secs rest after each exercise

(level 1 = 2x, level 2 = 4x, level 3 = 6x)

This slow reps then fast reps session is sure to have you reach new found gains and abilities. #nosurrender

Sumo Squat

fast

Bridge and Reach

Sumo Squat

slow

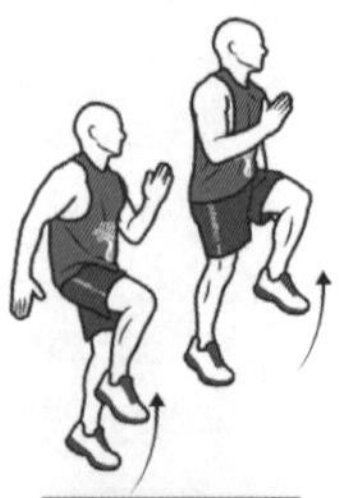

High Knees

fast

Bear Crawl

High Knees

slow

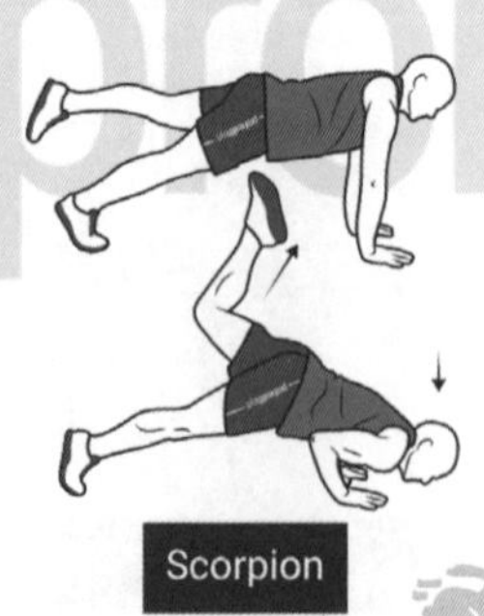

Scorpion

fast

YTWL

Scorpion

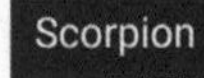

slow

Neck Check

10 of each exercise | rest after circuit

(level 1 = 1x, level 2 = 3x, level 3 = 5x)

This great neck range of motion routine will help fight neck pain and tightness... consider doing it 2-3x per day

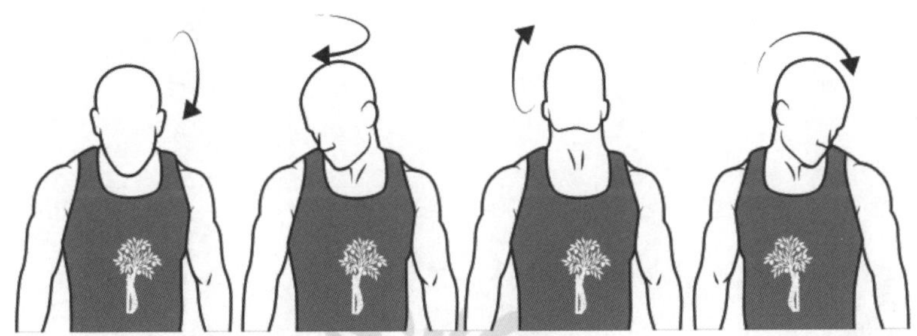

Ninja

40 secs ON | 20 secs rest after each exercise

(level 1 = 2x, level 2 = 5x, level 3 = 10x)

Be like a ninja, moving with strength, speed and stealth.
Have fun and say "I am the ninja."

Walking Toe Touches

fast

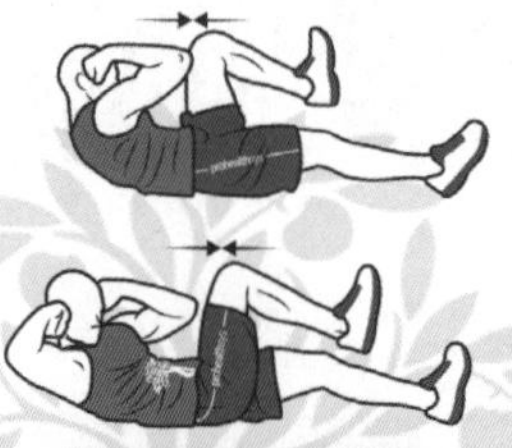

Bicycle Crunches

Walking Toe Touches

slow

Jumping Jacks

fast

Pike Push-Up

Jumping Jacks

slow

Playground

40 secs ON | 20 secs rest after each exercise

(level 1 = 2x, level 2 = 5x, level 3 = 10x)

It's time to play at the playground with a ball. Find happiness and remember your child like wonder with this fun routine.

Partner Press

10 of each exercise | rest after circuit

(level 1 = 2x, level 2 = 5x, level 3 = 10x)

This great butt burner will be sure to add more junk in your trunk... in a good way #bubblebutt ☺

Knee Raise Run

Pump

Push Up

Throwing Lunge

Partner Abs

Glute Hams

Pillow Fight

40 secs ON | 20 secs rest after each exercise

(level 1 = 2x, level 2 = 5x, level 3 = 10x)

Grab a pillow (or ball, back pack, bag, pot or even small kids/pets) and move them around in space

Side Plank

Dead Bug

Bird Dog

Static Lunge With Block Pass Through

Single Leg Bridge

Uneven Push-Ups

Plank IYTW

Power Pose

30 sec of each exercise

(level 1 = 2x, level 2 = 5x, level 3 = 7x)

Power poses are scientifically proven to improve your mood and performance... #strikeapose

Pull Push Lunge

no rest

(level 1 = 10 circuit, 2 = 15 circuits, 3 = 20)

Push, pull, lunge are the cornerstone of mass building and strengthening exercises

Chin-Ups

5 chin-ups

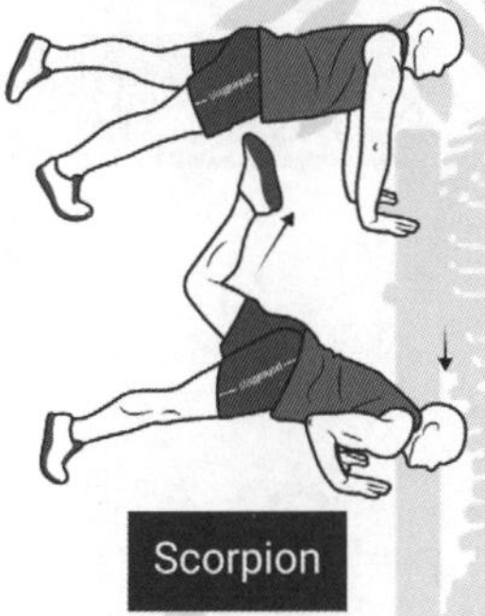

Scorpion

10 push-ups

Lunge

15 lunge

Quick HIIT

20 sec per exercise | no rest

(level 1 = 3 cycles, 2 = 6 cycles, 3 = 10 cycles)

Wicked joy with this lower body explosive power routine.

Jumping Jacks

Plank Rotations

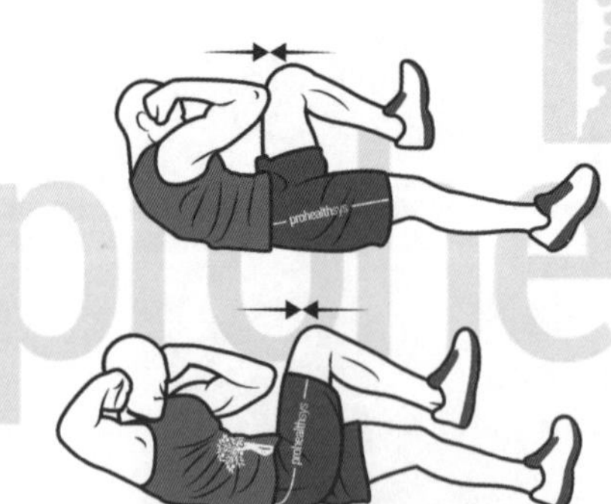

Bicycle Crunches

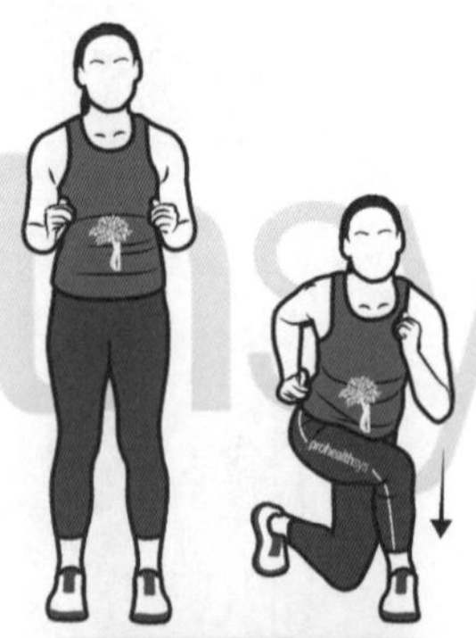

Curtsy Squat

Ragnarök

5-12 each exercise | controlled movement

(level 1 = 1 circuit, 2 = 3 circuits, 40 sec rest, 3 = 5 circuits, 30 sec rest)

Be like Thor, simplify your strength routine. These basic movements NEED to be OWNED movements to be functionally strong and avoid injury

Roll Out

20 sec per exercise | no rest

(level 1 = 2 cycles, 2 = 4 cycles, 3 = 5 cycles)

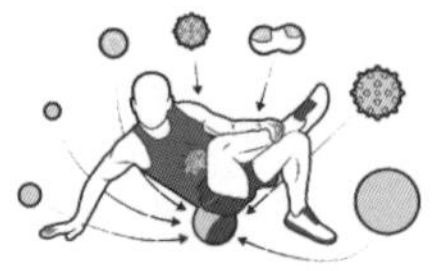

This foam roller inspired routine can be done anywhere you have space to get rolling!

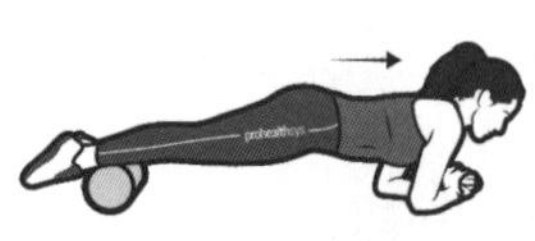

Plank

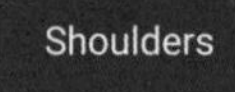

Shoulder Blade Reach

Lunge + Rotations

Thoracic Extension+ Side to Side

Knee & feet rotations

Single Leg Bridge

Rogue 1

8-12 of each exercise | rest after each

(level 1 = 2x, level 2 = 3x, level 3 = 5x)

This barbell inspired routine can easily help you build real muscle size and strength.

Overhead Squat

Deadlift

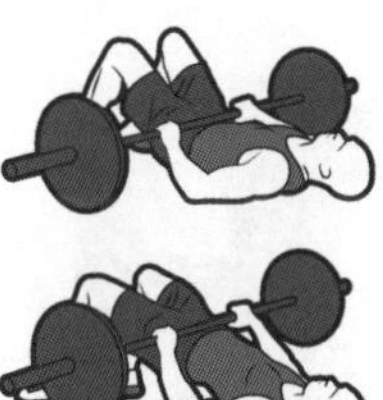

Glute Bridge

Shoulder Press

Bench Press

Pull-Up

Bent Over Row

Reps	Training Goal
2	
3	**STRENGTH** (3-5 sets, 3-5 reps)
4	
5	
6	
7	
8	
9	
10	**HYPERTROPHY** (3-4 sets, 8-12 reps)
11	
12	

Seated Yoga

30 sec per exercise with breath | no rest

(level 1 = 2 cycles, 2 = 4 cycles, 3 = 5 cycles)

Sit, breath and flow on the mat in a seated cycle of relaxation... you deserve it!

Cow

Cat

Extended Child's Pose

Garland

Comfortable Seat

Head-to-knee

Seated Twist

Pigeon

Cow Face

Super Plank

1 min per exercise | **1 min** rest

(level 1 = 1 circuit, 2 = 3 circuits, 40 sec rest, 3 = 5 circuits, 30 sec rest)

Become a plank tank with this core blasting circuit.

Strong Man

8-12 reps per exercise | 30 sec rest

(level 1 = 2 cycles, level 2 = 3 cycles, level 3 = 5 cycles)

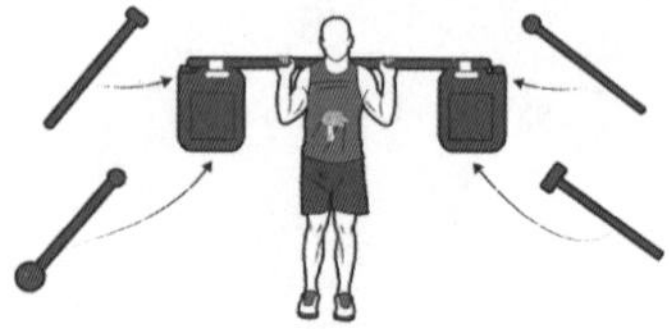

So you want to be a strong man? Back and Bi's... Chest and Tri's... Leg day... Get is all in this beasty session.

Close Grip Bench Press

Incline Bench Press

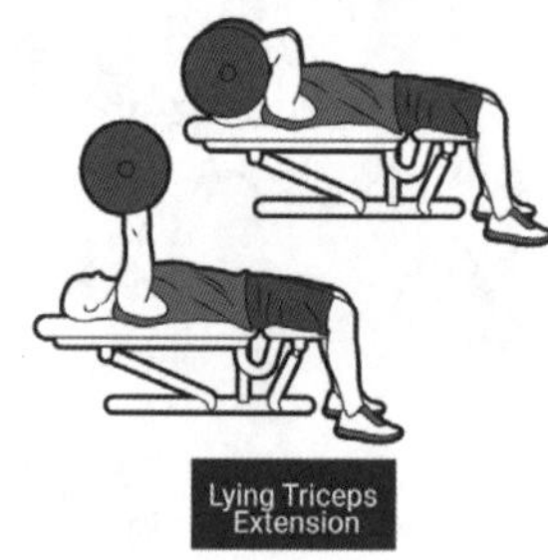

Lying Triceps Extension

Bicep Curl

T-Bar Row

Back Shrug

Landmine Front Squat

Suitcase Deadlift

Landmine Single Leg Deadlift

Sun Salutation

Cycle to breath | no rest

(level 1 = 2 cycles, 2 = 4 cycles, 3 = 5 cycles)

Vinyasa = Flow with breath - this flow is used by BILLIONS of people around the world to improve health.

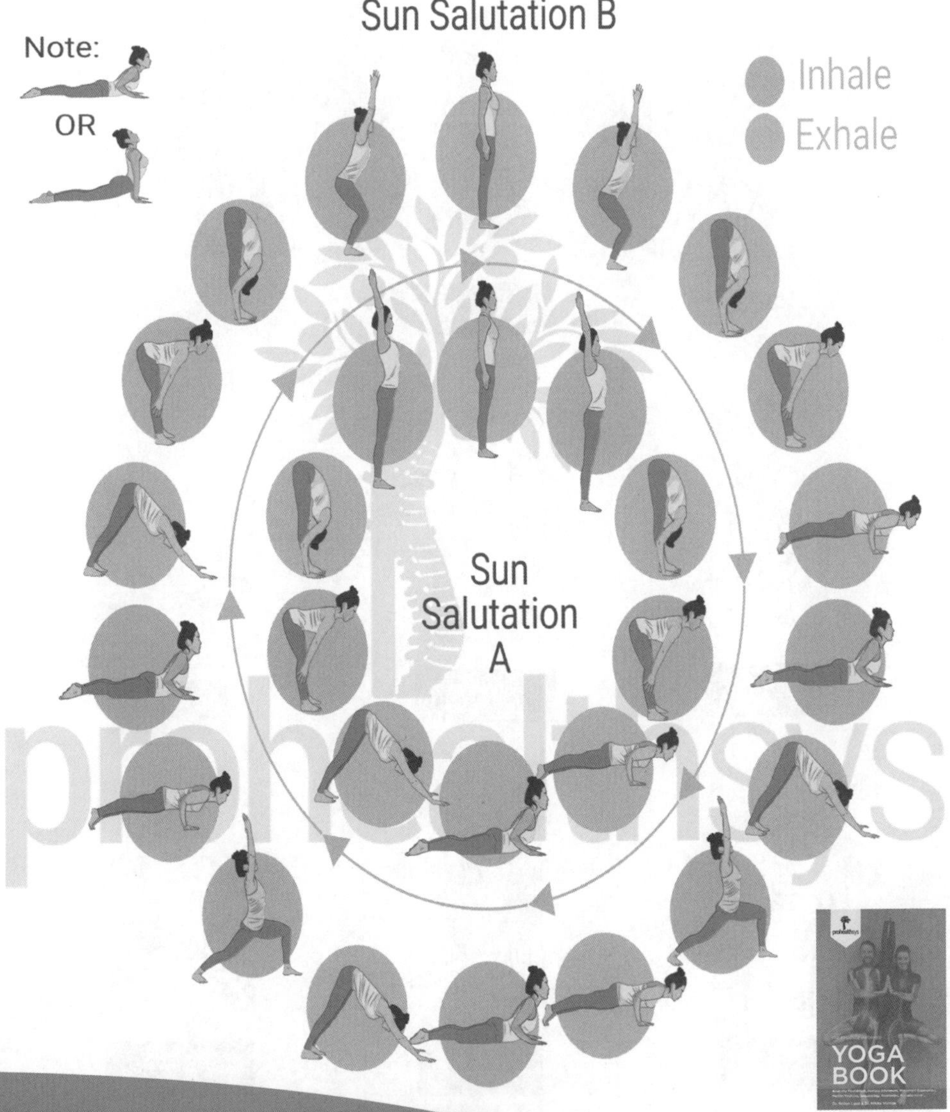

White Noise

40 sec per exercise | rest at end of cycle

(level 1 = 2 cycles, 2 = 4 cycles, 3 = 5 cycles)

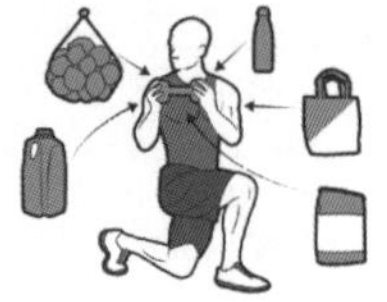

Wicked joy with this lower body explosive power routine.

Turkish Get-Ups

Double Arm Swing

Single Leg Scarecrow

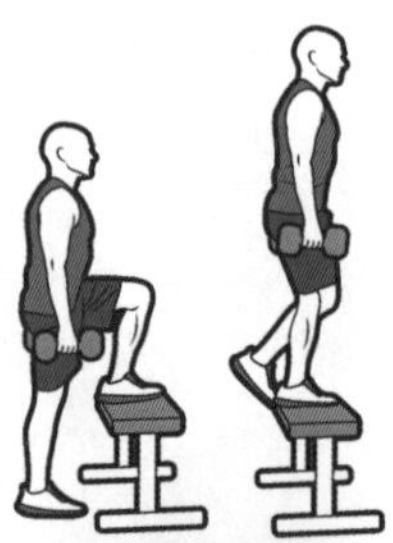

Step Up

Stance Switch Swing

Lunge and Rotation

Renegade Row

X-rated

Time varies based on skill and ability

(level 1 = 1 circuit, 2 = 3 circuits, 3 = 5+ circuits)

Welcome to another fun partners routine. There are even more options shown in the back section... #superfun

Yes U Can

Basic Acrobatics

You may never have done this before, but yes you can.

spinal twist

whirlpool

double chair
same leg

double chair
opposite leg

partner chair

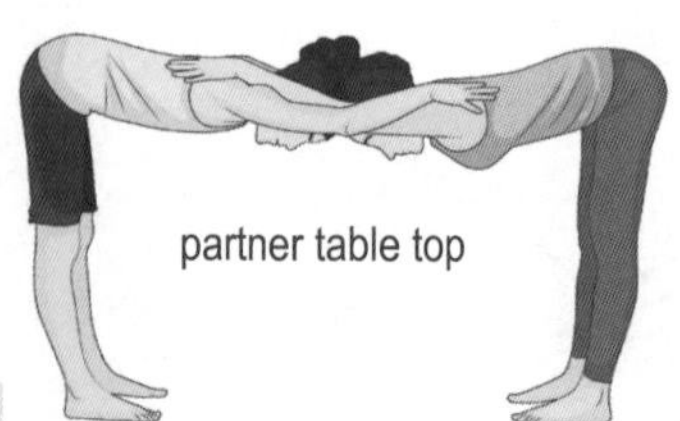

partner table top

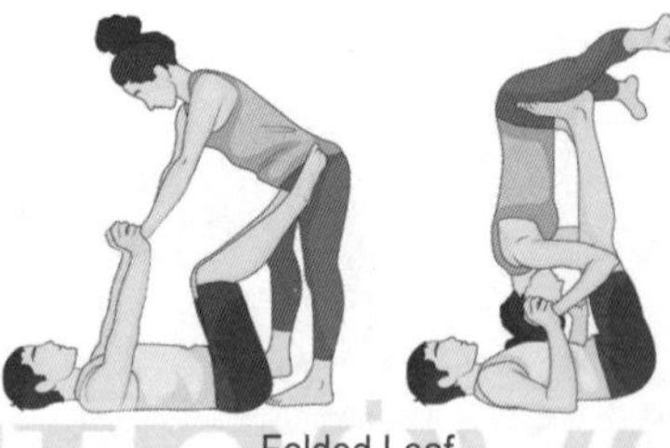

Folded Leaf

Start (dismount is reverse)

back fly

Zone 2

40 sec per exercise | rest after cycle

(level 1 = 2 cycles, 2 = 4 cycles, 3 = 5 cycles)

Suspension gyms are a great way to mix up your routine. They take up minimal space and are portable. You can even use sheets in a pinch

□ 40 sec on/20 off, □ pyramid, □ 8-12 of each

(level 1 = 2 cycles, 2 = 4 cycles, 3 = 5 cycles)

Make your own fun for personalized health and fitness

"The only limit is your imagination."

□ ___ sec on/___ rest, □ pyramid, □ ____ reps

(level 1 = 2 cycles, 2 = 4 cycles, 3 = 5 cycles)

Make your own fun for personalized health and fitness

"The only limit is your imagination."

Make your own circuit: **Circle and do your Top 5**

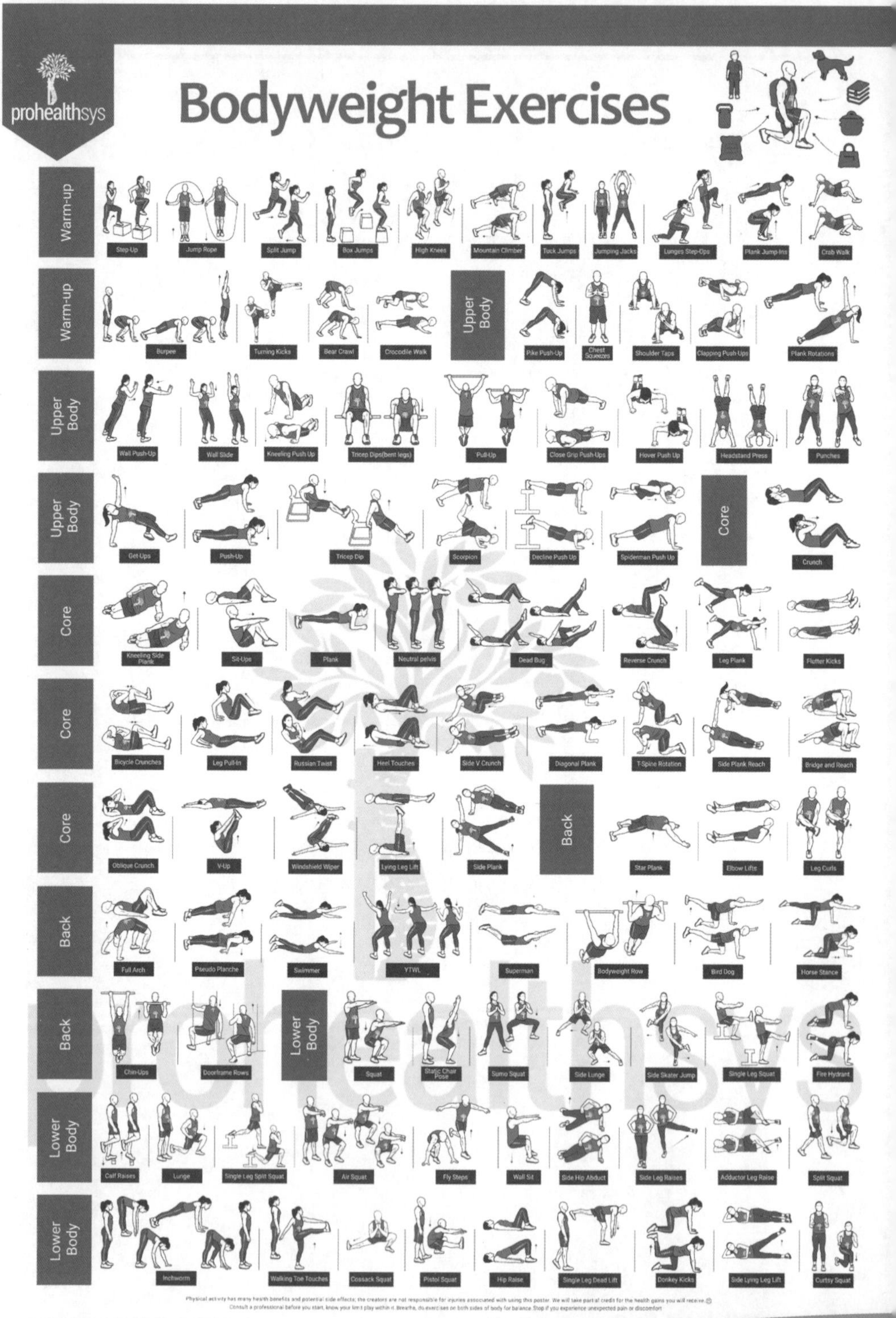

Bodyweight Exercises

Warm-up
Step-Up · Jump Rope · Split Jump · Box Jumps · High Knees · Mountain Climber · Tuck Jumps · Jumping Jacks · Lunges Step-Ops · Plank Jump-Ins · Crab Walk

Warm-up
Burpee · Turning Kicks · Bear Crawl · Crocodile Walk

Upper Body
Pike Push-Up · Chest Squeezes · Shoulder Taps · Clapping Push-Ups · Plank Rotations

Upper Body
Wall Push-Up · Wall Slide · Kneeling Push Up · Tricep Dips(bent legs) · Pull-Up · Close Grip Push-Ups · Hover Push Up · Headstand Press · Punches

Upper Body
Get-Ups · Push-Up · Tricep Dip · Scorpion · Decline Push Up · Spiderman Push Up

Core
Crunch

Core
Kneeling Side Plank · Sit-Ups · Plank · Neutral pelvis · Dead Bug · Reverse Crunch · Leg Plank · Flutter Kicks

Core
Bicycle Crunches · Leg Pull-In · Russian Twist · Heel Touches · Side V Crunch · Diagonal Plank · T-Spine Rotation · Side Plank Reach · Bridge and Reach

Core
Oblique Crunch · V-Up · Windshield Wiper · Lying Leg Lift · Side Plank

Back
Star Plank · Elbow Lifts · Leg Curls

Back
Full Arch · Pseudo Planche · Swimmer · YTWL · Superman · Bodyweight Row · Bird Dog · Horse Stance

Back
Chin-Ups · Doorframe Rows

Lower Body
Squat · Static Chair Pose · Sumo Squat · Side Lunge · Side Skater Jump · Single Leg Squat · Fire Hydrant

Lower Body
Calf Raises · Lunge · Single Leg Split Squat · Air Squat · Fly Steps · Wall Sit · Side Hip Abduct · Side Leg Raises · Adductor Leg Raise · Split Squat

Lower Body
Inchworm · Walking Toe Touches · Cossack Squat · Pistol Squat · Hip Raise · Single Leg Dead Lift · Donkey Kicks · Side Lying Leg Lift · Curtsy Squat

Physical activity has many health benefits and potential side effects; the creators are not responsible for injuries associated with using this poster. We will take partial credit for the health gains you will receive.
Consult a professional before you start, know your limit play within it. Breathe, do exercises on both sides of body for balance. Stop if you experience unexpected pain or discomfort.

Huge wall poster available

Make your own circuit: **Circle and do your Top 5**

Barbell Exercises

Category	Exercises
Upper body	Close Grip Bench Press; Bicep Curl; Bench Press; Shoulder Press; Reverse Bicep Curl; Pull Over
Upper body	Incline Bench Press; Decline Bench Press; Overhead Press; Landmine Overhead Press; Front Raise; Kickback
Upper Body	Lying Triceps Extension; Push Press; Press Behind Neck; Close-Grip Upright Row; Wrist Curl; One Arm Shoulder Press
Core	Russian Twist; Roll Out; Overhead Sit-Up; Barbell Wipers; Side Crunch; Zercher Carry
Back	Bent Over Row
Back	Drag Curl; Landmine Row; Shrug; Back Shrug; T-Bar Row; Pinch Grip Deadlift
Lower Body	Side Lunge; Calf Raises; Glute Hamstring Raise; Single-Arm Shoulder Press; Front Squat; Barbell Clean
Lower Body	Back Squat; Deadlift; Front Lunge; Landmine Front Squat; Romanian Deadlift; Overhead Lunge
Lower Body	Suitcase Deadlift; Bulgarian Split Squat; Good Morning; Landmine Single Leg Deadlift; Hip Thrust; Overhead Squat
Lower Body	Sumo Deadlift; Hang Clean and Press; Squat and Press; Glute Bridge; Split Squat; Squat Jumps

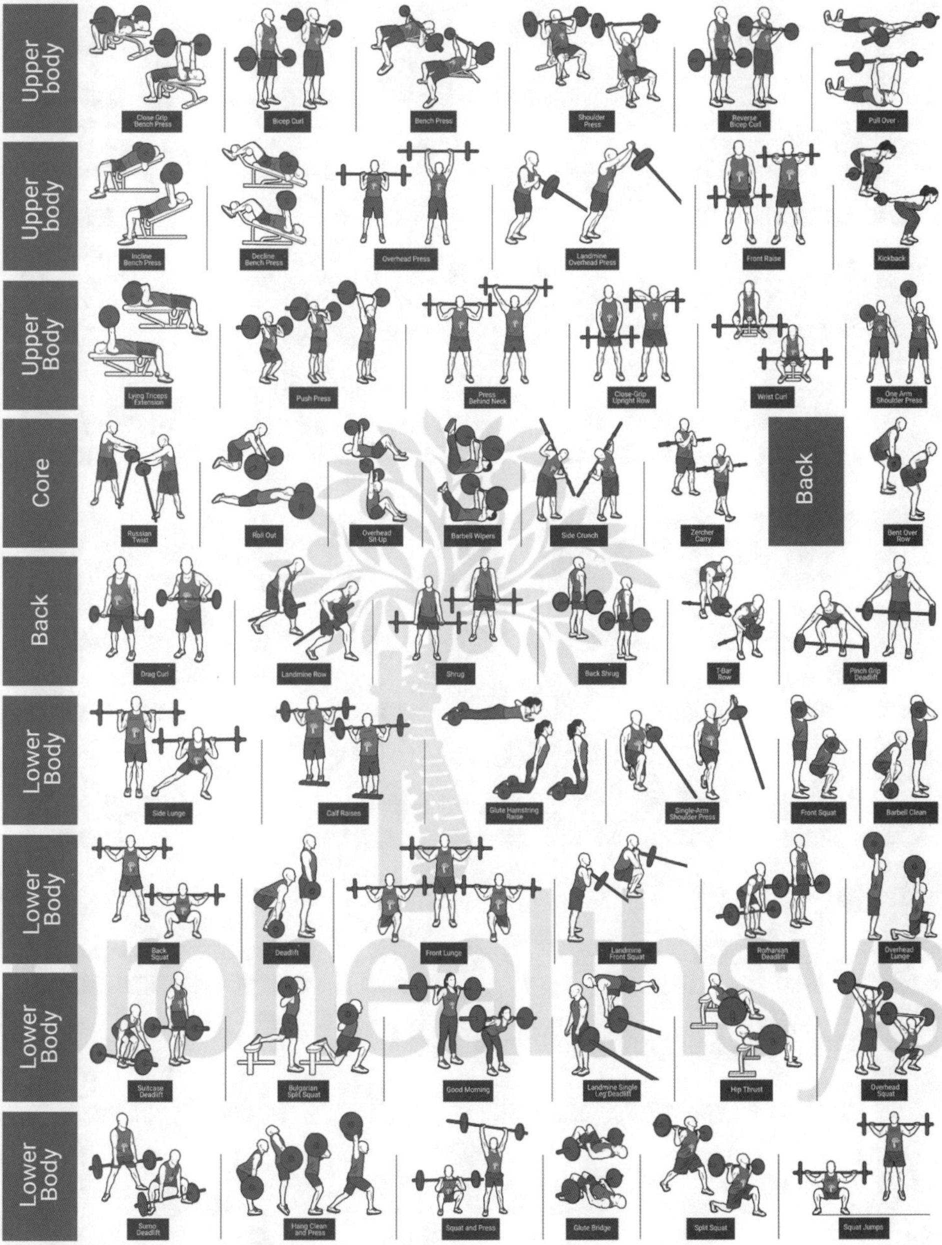

Physical activity has many health benefits and potential side effects; the creators are not responsible for injuries associated with using this poster. We will take partial credit for the health gains you will receive. ☺
Consult a professional before you start, know your limit play within it. Breathe, do exercises on both sides of body for balance. Stop if you experience unexpected pain or discomfort

Make your own circuit: **Circle and do your Top 5**

Body Ball Exercises

Entire Body
- Ball Transfer
- Alt.Arm & Leg Lift

Upper Body
- Chest Press
- Incline Chest Press
- One-Arm Chest Press

Upper Body
- Decline Push-up
- Incline Push-up
- Tricep Dip
- Tricep Extension
- Chest Fly
- Lat Pullover

Upper Body
- External Shoulder Rotation
- Knee Push-Ups
- Shoulder Press
- Tricep Kickback

Core
- Russian Twist
- Pike Crunch

Core
- Twist Crunch
- Plank Shoulder Taps
- Side Plank
- Roll-in Roll-out
- Ball Leg Lift
- Knee Raises
- Basic Rollout

Core
- Ab Rollout
- Table Tops
- Jackknife
- Oblique Crunch
- Alternating Crossover
- Raised Feet Sit-up
- Crunch

Core
- Plank
- Twisting Knee Tuck
- Crunch Legs on Ball

Back
- Back Extension
- Prone Cobra
- Superman
- Reverse Fly

Back
- Pelvic Tilts
- Lateral Pelvic Tilts

Lower Body
- Squeeze, Curl & Lift
- Side Leg Raise
- Hip Raise
- Hip Extension

Lower Body
- Squat
- Knee Tuck
- Butt Blaster
- Single Leg Split Squat
- Hamstring Curl
- Kneeling Ball Squeeze
- Side Leg Lift

Lower Body
- Inner Thigh Ball Squeeze
- Standing Side Leg Push
- Hamstring Squeeze
- Toe Pulls
- Standing Calf
- Mountain Climber

Lower Body
- Single Leg Bridge
- Straight Leg Deadbug
- Knee To Chest
- Stability Supine Leg Twists

Physical activity has many health benefits and potential side effects; the creators are not responsible for injuries associated with using this poster. We will take partial credit for the health gains you will receive. ☺ Consult a professional before you start, know your limit play within it. Breathe, do exercises on both sides of body for balance. Stop if you experience unexpected pain or discomfort.

Make your own circuit: **Circle and do your Top 5**

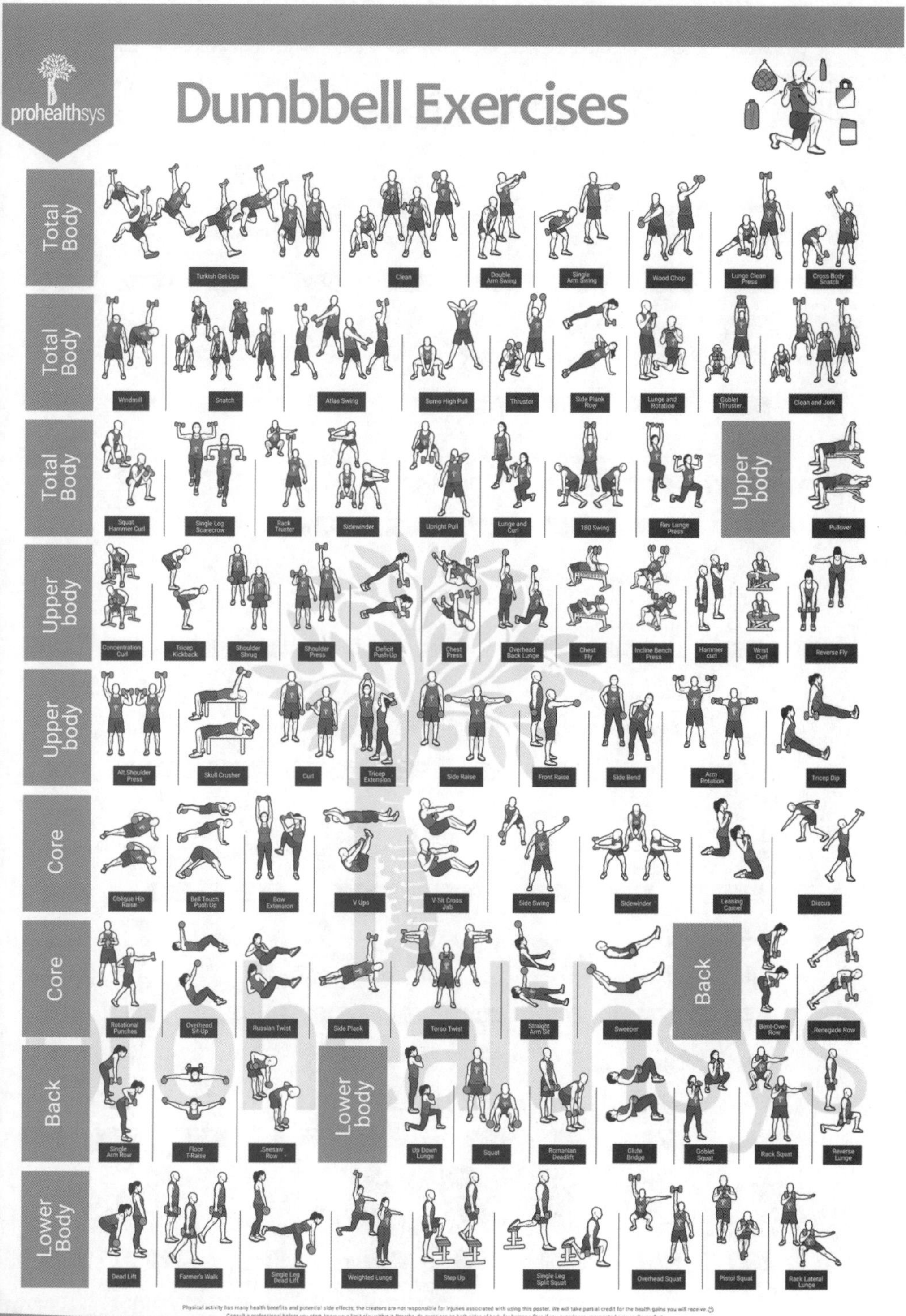

Dumbbell Exercises

Total Body

Turkish Get-Ups · Clean · Double Arm Swing · Single Arm Swing · Wood Chop · Lunge Clean Press · Cross Body Snatch

Total Body

Windmill · Snatch · Atlas Swing · Sumo High Pull · Thruster · Side Plank Row · Lunge and Rotation · Goblet Thruster · Clean and Jerk

Total Body

Squat Hammer Curl · Single Leg Scarecrow · Rack Truster · Sidewinder · Upright Pull · Lunge and Curl · 180 Swing · Rev Lunge Press

Upper body

Pullover

Upper body

Concentration Curl · Tricep Kickback · Shoulder Shrug · Shoulder Press · Deficit Push-Up · Chest Press · Overhead Back Lunge · Chest Fly · Incline Bench Press · Hammer curl · Wrist Curl · Reverse Fly

Upper body

Alt Shoulder Press · Skull Crusher · Curl · Tricep Extension · Side Raise · Front Raise · Side Bend · Arm Rotation · Tricep Dip

Core

Oblique Hip Raise · Bell Touch Push Up · Bow Extension · V Ups · V-Sit Cross Jab · Side Swing · Sidewinder · Leaning Camel · Discus

Core

Rotational Punches · Overhead Sit-Up · Russian Twist · Side Plank · Torso Twist · Straight Arm Sit · Sweeper

Back

Bent-Over-Row · Renegade Row

Back

Single Arm Row · Floor T-Raise · Seesaw Row

Lower body

Up Down Lunge · Squat · Romanian Deadlift · Glute Bridge · Goblet Squat · Rack Squat · Reverse Lunge

Lower Body

Dead Lift · Farmer's Walk · Single Leg Dead Lift · Weighted Lunge · Step Up · Single Leg Split Squat · Overhead Squat · Pistol Squat · Rack Lateral Lunge

Physical activity has many health benefits and potential side effects; the creators are not responsible for injuries associated with using this poster. We will take partial credit for the health gains you will receive ☺
Consult a professional before you start, know your limit play within it. Breathe, do exercises on both sides of body for balance. Stop if you experience unexpected pain or discomfort

Make your own circuit: **Circle and do your Top 5**

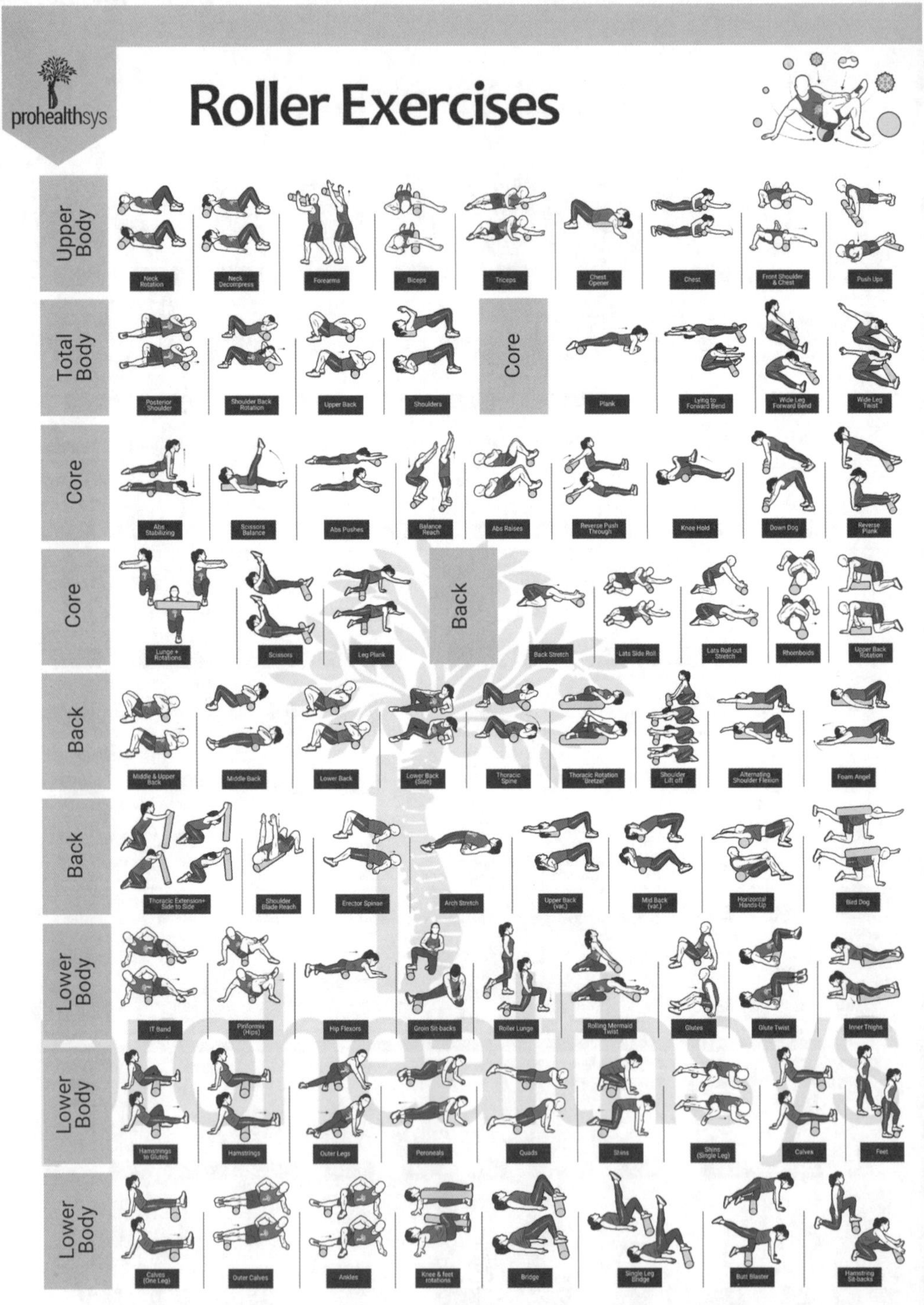

Roller Exercises

Upper Body: Neck Rotation · Neck Decompress · Forearms · Biceps · Triceps · Chest Opener · Chest · Front Shoulder & Chest · Push Ups

Total Body: Posterior Shoulder · Shoulder Back Rotation · Upper Back · Shoulders

Core: Plank · Lying to Forward Bend · Wide Leg Forward Bend · Wide Leg Twist

Core: Abs Stabilizing · Scissors Balance · Abs Pushes · Balance Reach · Abs Raises · Reverse Push Through · Knee Hold · Down Dog · Reverse Plank

Core: Lunge + Rotations · Scissors · Leg Plank

Back: Back Stretch · Lats Side Roll · Lats Roll-out Stretch · Rhomboids · Upper Back Rotation

Back: Middle & Upper Back · Middle Back · Lower Back · Lower Back (Side) · Thoracic Spine · Thoracic Rotation Bretzel · Shoulder Lift off · Alternating Shoulder Flexion · Foam Angel

Back: Thoracic Extension+ Side to Side · Shoulder Blade Reach · Erector Spinae · Arch Stretch · Upper Back (var.) · Mid Back (var.) · Horizontal Hands-Up · Bird Dog

Lower Body: IT Band · Piriformis (Hips) · Hip Flexors · Groin Sit-backs · Roller Lunge · Rolling Mermaid Twist · Glutes · Glute Twist · Inner Thighs

Lower Body: Hamstrings to Glutes · Hamstrings · Outer Legs · Peroneals · Quads · Shins · Shins (Single Leg) · Calves · Feet

Lower Body: Calves (One Leg) · Outer Calves · Ankles · Knee & feet rotations · Bridge · Single Leg Bridge · Butt Blaster · Hamstring Sit-backs

Make your own circuit: **Circle and do your Top 5**

Kettle Bell Exercises

Total Body
Turkish Get-Ups · Clean · Double Arm Swing · Single Arm Swing · Wood Chop · Lunge Clean Press · Cross Body Snatch

Total Body
Windmill · Snatch · Atlas Swing · Sumo High Pull · Thruster · Side Plank Row · Vertical Pull · Goblet Thruster · Clean and Jerk

Total Body
Squat Knee · Ribbons · Rack Truster · Sidewinder · Upright Pull · Sit Up Press · 180 Swing · Stance Switch Swing

Upper body
Russian Swing

Upper body
Shoulder Toss · Cross Body Swing · Goblet Curl · Shoulder Press · Deficit Push-Up · Chest Press · Overhead Back Lunge · Goblet Squat Curl · Rack Push Press · Hammer curl · Crossfit Swing · One Arm Russian Swing

Upper body
Pull-Over · Halo · Curl · Tricep Extension · Side Raise · Front Raise · Side Bend · Goblet Press · Front Circle · Tricep Dip

Core
Oblique Hip Raise · Bell Touch Push Up · Leg Raise · Plyo Push up · Criss Cross Swing · Side Swing · Sidewinder · Around-the-Body · Figure Eight

Core
Half Turkish Get-Up · Overhead Sit-Up · Russian Twist · Side Plank · Torso Twist · Straight Arm Sit · Seated Oblique Swing

Back
Bent-Over-Row · Renegade Row

Back
Single Arm Row

Lower body
Rack Lateral Lunge · Goblet Lateral Squat · Up Down Lunge · Side Lunge · Bob and Weave · Goblet Squat · Rack Squat · Good Morning

Lower Body
Dead Lift · Farmer's Walk · Single Leg Dead Lift · Weighted Lunge · Lunge Pass · Squat · Squat Flip · Overhead Squat · Pistol Squat

Physical activity has many health benefits and potential side effects; the creators are not responsible for injuries associated with using this poster. We will take partial credit for the health gains you will receive ☺
Consult a professional before you start, know your limit play within it. Breathe, do exercises on both sides of body for balance. Stop if you experience unexpected pain or discomfort.

Huge wall poster available

Make your own circuit: **Circle and do your Top 5**

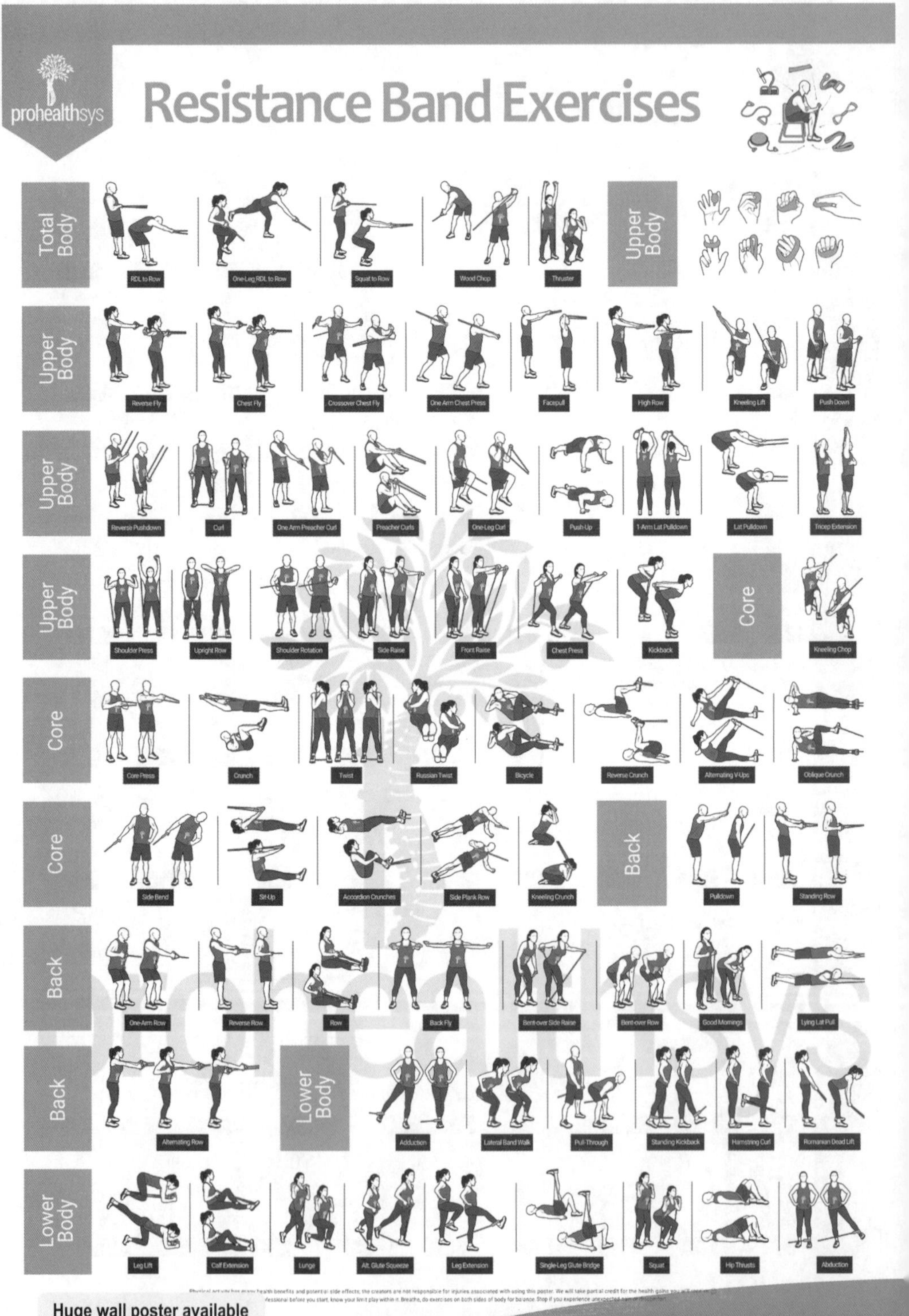

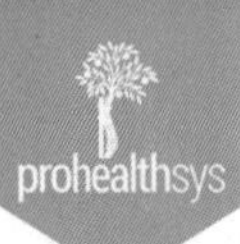

prohealthsys
Resistance Band Exercises
Total Body
RDL to Row
One-Leg RDL to Row
Squat to Row
Wood Chop
Thruster
Upper Body
Upper Body
Reverse Fly
Chest Fly
Crossover Chest Fly
One Arm Chest Press
Facepull
High Row
Kneeling Lift
Push Down
Upper Body
Reverse Pushdown
Curl
One Arm Preacher Curl
Preacher Curls
One-Leg Curl
Push Up
1-Arm Lat Pulldown
Lat Pulldown
Tricep Extension
Upper Body
Shoulder Press
Upright Row
Shoulder Rotation
Side Raise
Front Raise
Chest Press
Kickback
Core
Kneeling Chop
Core
Core Press
Crunch
Twist
Russian Twist
Bicycle
Reverse Crunch
Alternating V-Ups
Oblique Crunch
Core
Side Bend
Sit-Up
Accordion Crunches
Side Plank Row
Kneeling Crunch
Back
Pulldown
Standing Row
Back
One-Arm Row
Reverse Row
Row
Back Fly
Bent-over Side Raise
Bent-over Row
Good Mornings
Lying Lat Pull
Back
Alternating Row
Lower Body
Adduction
Lateral Band Walk
Pull-Through
Standing Kickback
Hamstring Curl
Romanian Dead Lift
Lower Body
Leg Lift
Calf Extension
Lunge
Alt. Glute Squeeze
Leg Extension
Single-Leg Glute Bridge
Squat
Hip Thrusts
Abduction

Huge wall poster available

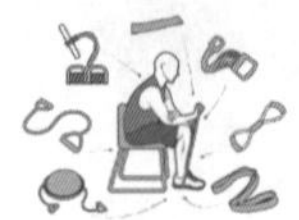

Make your own circuit: **Circle and do your Top 5**

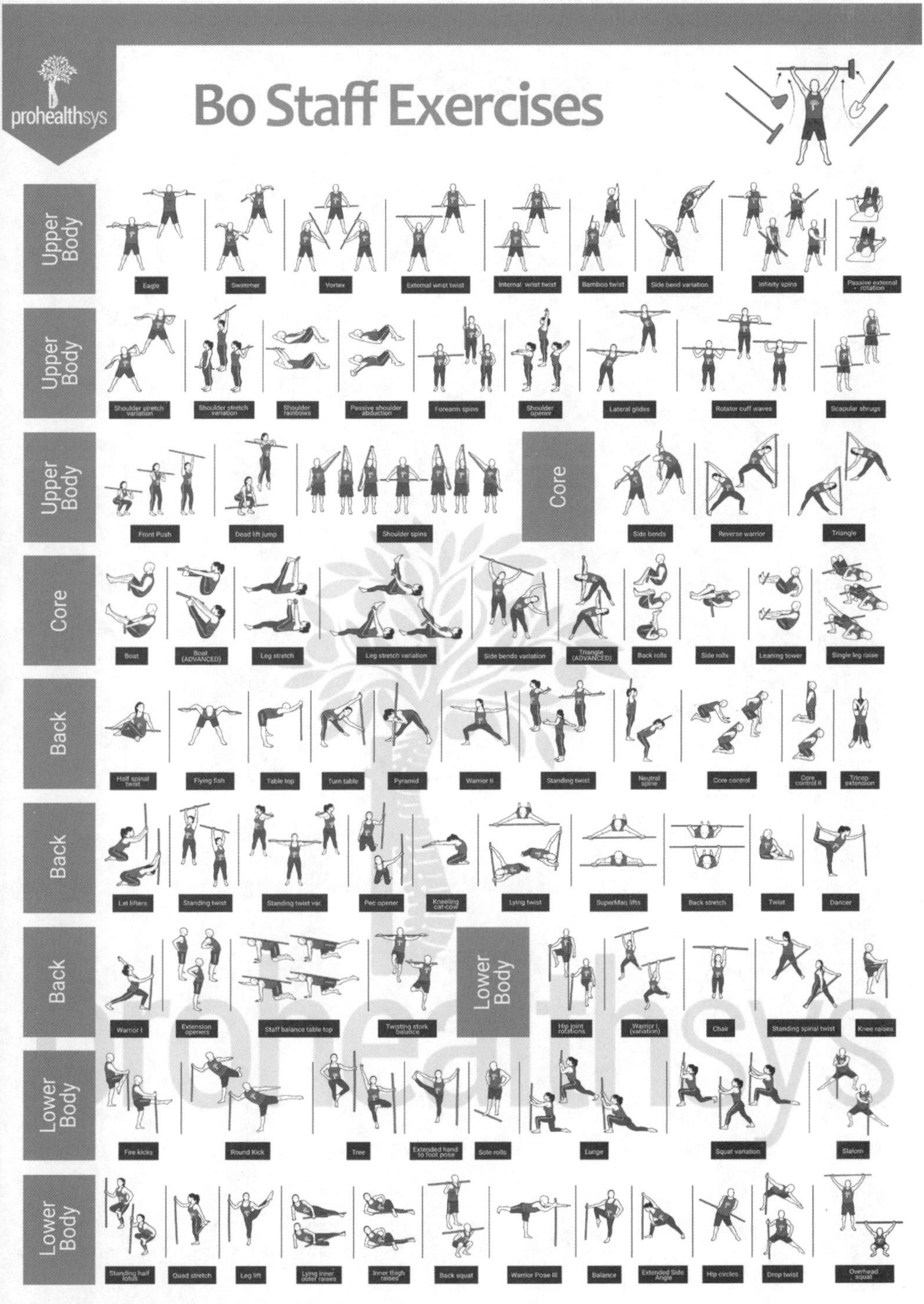

Bo Staff Exercises

Upper Body
Eagle · Swimmer · Vortex · External wrist twist · Internal wrist twist · Bamboo twist · Side bend variation · Infinity spins · Passive external rotation

Upper Body
Shoulder stretch variation · Shoulder stretch variation · Shoulder rainbows · Passive shoulder abduction · Forearm spins · Shoulder opener · Lateral glides · Rotator cuff waves · Scapular shrugs

Upper Body
Front Push · Dead lift jump · Shoulder spins

Core
Side bends · Reverse warrior · Triangle

Core
Boat · Boat (ADVANCED) · Leg stretch · Leg stretch variation · Side bends variation · Triangle (ADVANCED) · Back rolls · Side rolls · Leaning tower · Single leg raise

Back
Half spinal twist · Flying fish · Table top · Turn table · Pyramid · Warrior II · Standing twist · Neutral spine · Core control · Core control II · Tricep extension

Back
Lat lifters · Standing twist · Standing twist var. · Pec opener · Kneeling cat-cow · Lying twist · SuperMan lifts · Back stretch · Twist · Dancer

Back
Warrior I · Extension openers · Staff balance table top · Twisting stork balance

Lower Body
Hip joint rotations · Warrior I (variation) · Chair · Standing spinal twist · Knee raises

Lower Body
Fire kicks · Round Kick · Tree · Extended hand to foot pose · Sole rolls · Lunge · Squat variation · Slalom

Lower Body
Standing half lotus · Quad stretch · Leg lift · Lying inner outer raises · Inner thigh raises · Back squat · Warrior Pose III · Balance · Extended Side Angle · Hip circles · Drop twist · Overhead squat

Make your own circuit: **Circle and do your Top 5**

Stretching Strap

Upper Body

Upper Body

Core

Core

Back

Back

Back

Lower Body

Lower Body

Lower Body

Lower Body

Mobilization

Make your own circuit: **Circle and do your Top 5**

Stretching Exercises

Forearms

Forearms

Shoulders

Shoulders

Shoulders

Shoulders

Neck

Neck

Torso

Torso

Torso

Torso

Hips

Hips

Hips

Glutes, Quads

Glutes, Quads

Hamstrings

Hamstrings

Ankles, Calves

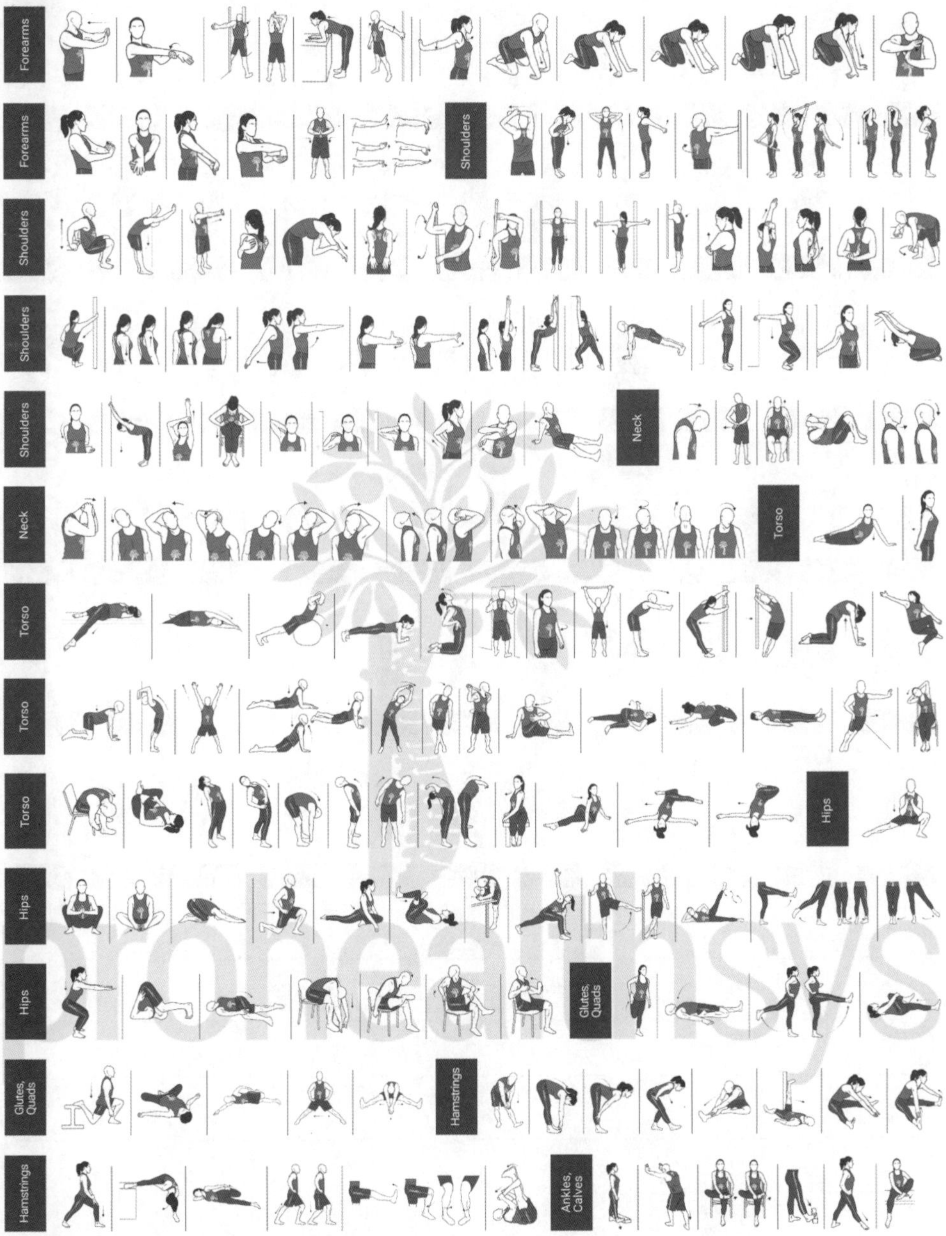

Physical activity has many health benefits and potential side effects, the creators are not responsible for injuries associated with using this poster. We will take partial credit for the health gains you will receive ☺
Consult a professional before you start, know your limit play within it. Breathe, do exercises on both sides of body for balance. Stop if you experience unexpected pain or discomfort

Taichi Exercises

Starting | Opening | Part the Wild Horse's | Part the Wild Horse's Mane Left | Part the Wild Horse's Mane Right | Part the Wild Horse's Mane Left | White Crane Spreads Its Wings | Brush knee and Twist Steps Right | Brush Knee and Twist Steps Left | Brush Knee and Twist Steps (Right) | Play the Pipa (Right)

Repulse the monkey (Right) | Reverse Reeling Forearm(Right) | Step Back and Repulse Monkey (Left) | Hold the Ball | Grasp Sparrow's Tail (Left) | Grasp the Bird's Tail (Left) | Ward Off (Left) | Separate (Left) | Rollback (Left) | Push (Left) | Withdraw

Grasp Sparrow's Tail (Right) | Grasp the Bird's Tail (Right) | Ward Off (Right) | Rollback(Right) | Push(Right) | Single whip(Left) | Wave Hands Like Clouds | Cloud Hands(Left) | Single whip | High Pat on Horse | Step Up to Examine Horse

Separate Right Foot(Right) | Kick with Right Foot(Right) | Strike to Ears with Both Fists | Turn Body | Separate Left Foot | Left Heel Kick | Single Whip Squatting Down (Left) | Snake Creeps Down (Left) | Golden Rooster Stands on One Leg (Left) | Golden Bird Standing Alone (Left) | Single Whip Squatting Down (Right)

Snake Creeps Down (Right) | Lower Single Whip Squatting Down | Golden Rooster Stands on One Leg (Right) | Golden Bird Standing Alone (Right) | Shuttle | Fair lady play with shuttle (Left) | Shuttle | Fair lady play with shuttle (Right) | Needle at Sea Bottom | Fan through back | Fan Penetrates Back

Turn Body | Deflect | Parry | Punch | Apparent Close | Withdraw | Push | Cross Hands | Conclusion | Closing | Start position

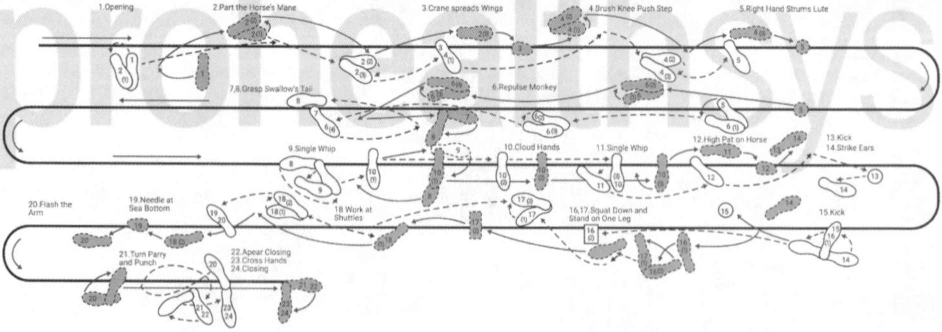

1.Opening
2.Part the Horse's Mane
3.Crane spreads Wings
4.Brush Knee Push Step
5.Right Hand Strums Lute
6.Repulse Monkey
7,8.Grasp Swallow's Tail
9.Single Whip
10.Cloud Hands
11.Single Whip
12.High Pat on Horse
13.Kick
14.Strike Ears
15.Kick
16,17.Squat Down and Stand on One Leg
18 Work at Shuttles
19.Needle at Sea Bottom
20.Flash the Arm
21.Turn Parry and Punch
22.Apear Closing
23.Cross Hands
24.Closing

Physical activity has many health benefits and potential side effects, the creators are not responsible for injuries associated with using this poster. We will take partial credit for the health gains you will receive.
Consult a professional before you start, know your limit play within it. Breathe, do exercises on both sides of body for balance. Stop if you experience unexpected pain or discomfort

Make your own circuit: **Circle and do your Top 5-10**

Suspension Exercises

Total Body
- Burpee
- Twist Row
- Santa Rows
- Pull-up & Straddle Over
- Lunge to I Fly
- Squat w/Crossover
- Spiderman Push-up
- Long Torso Twist

Total Body
- Sprinter Start
- Split Squat Y Fly
- Squat Y Fly
- Wide Stance Hip Hinge to Cossack

Upper Body
- Chest Fly
- Tricep Dip
- Tricep Press
- Push-up
- Curl

Upper Body
- Pull-up
- Tricep Push-up
- Shoulder Rotation
- Chest Press
- Incline Push-up
- Incline Press
- Handstand
- One Arm Row
- Clutch Curl
- Crossing Clutch Curl

Upper body
- One Arm Curl
- One Arm Chest Press
- Clock Press
- L Sit Pull-up
- Upper Back Stretch
- Kneeling Oblique Rollout

Core
- Crunches
- Plank
- Pike

Core
- Side Plank Tap
- Kneeling Roll-out
- Reverse Plank
- Oblique Crunch
- Pendulum
- Seesaw
- Torso Rotation
- Knee-to-chest
- Sit-up
- Standing Hip-drop

Core
- Side Plank & Reach
- Single Leg Plank
- Teaser
- Limbo
- Arm Walk
- Scorpion
- Hanging Wipers
- Atomic Push-Up
- Single-Leg Plank with Alternating Elbow Tap

Core
- Lat Pullover
- Power Pull
- Row
- Inverted row
- Rear Delt Fly
- Y Fly
- Lat Pull-down
- Alligator
- Camel Stretch

Lower Body
- Hamstring Curl
- Good Morning
- Hamstring Runners
- Suspended Lunge
- Squat
- Single Leg Squat
- Mountain Climber
- Split
- Knee-drive Jump
- Lower back Stretch with Rotations

Lower Body
- Step-over Side Lunge
- Suspended Side Lunge
- Single Leg Dead Lift
- Lunge Swing
- Overhead Squat
- Squat Jump
- Lunge Jump
- Hinge
- Figure 4 Stretch

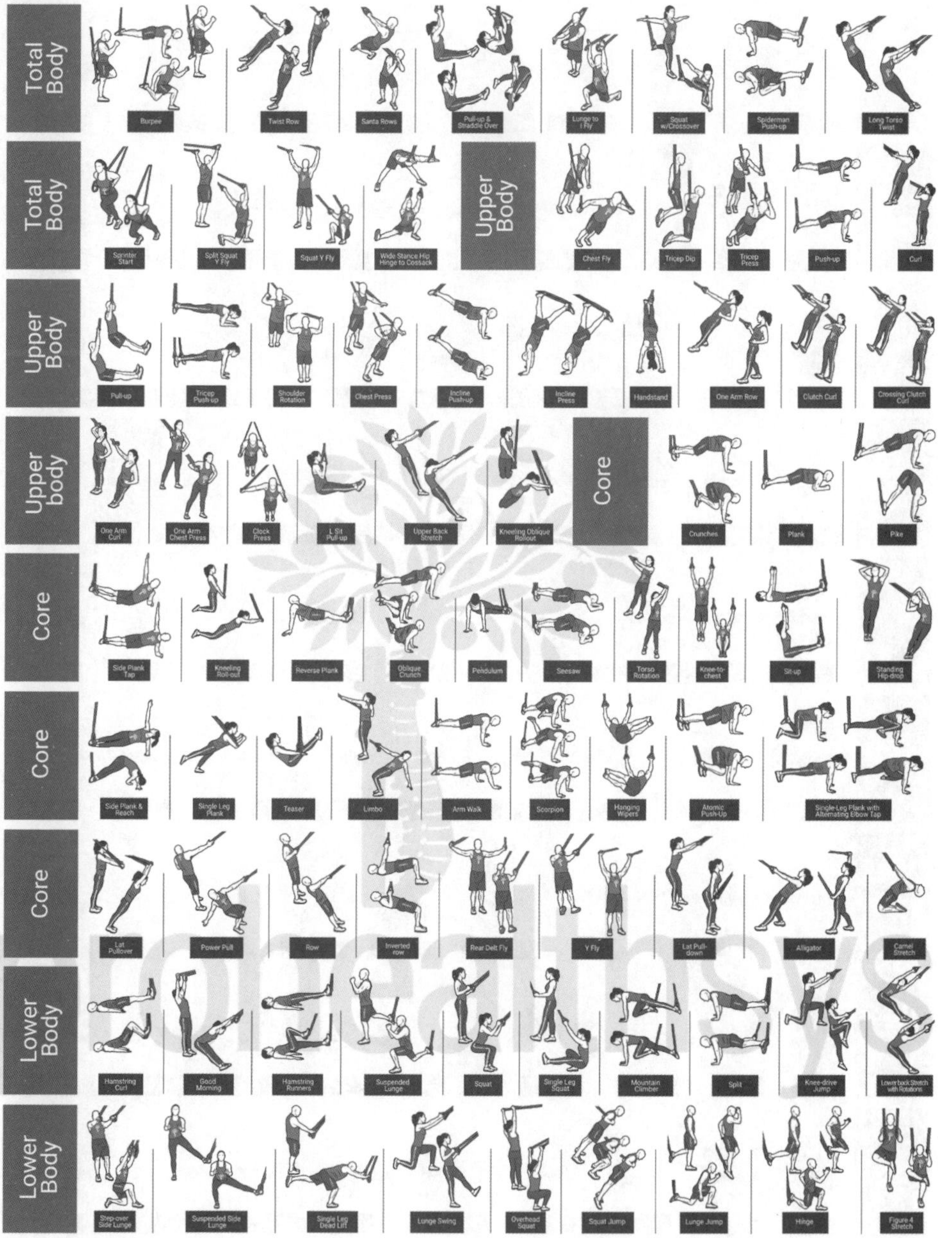

Physical activity has many health benefits and potential side effects, the creators are not responsible for injuries associated with using this poster. We will take partial credit for the health gains you will receive ☺
Consult a professional before you start, know your limit play within it. Breathe, do exercises on both sides of body for balance. Stop if you experience unexpected pain or discomfort

Make your own circuit: **Circle and do your Top 5**

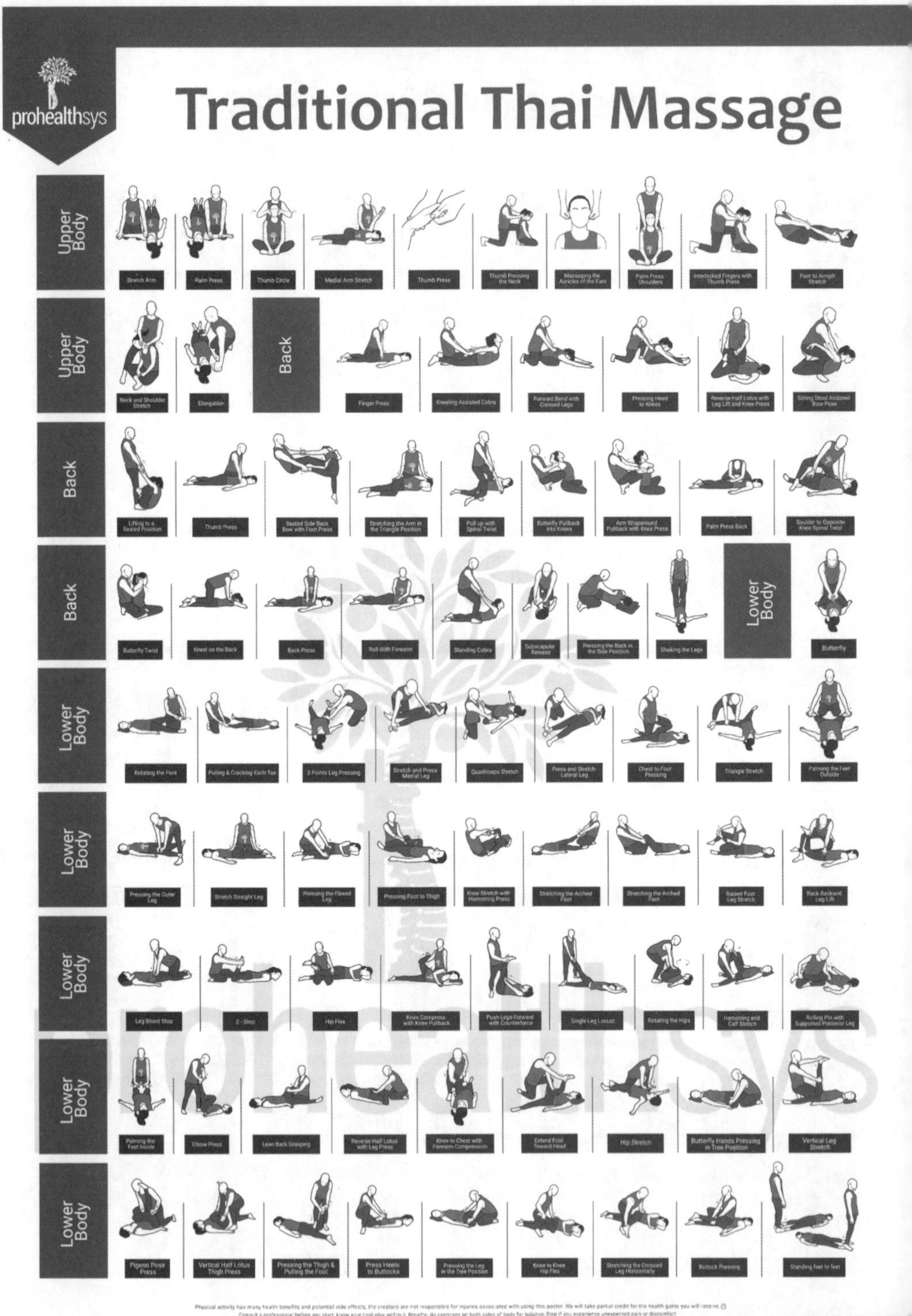

Traditional Thai Massage

Upper Body

Stretch Arm | Palm Press | Thumb Circle | Medial Arm Stretch | Thumb Press | Thumb Pressing the Neck | Massaging the Auricles of the Ears | Palm Press Shoulders | Interlocked Fingers with Thumb Press | Foot to Armpit Stretch

Upper Body

Neck and Shoulder Stretch | Elongation

Back

Finger Press | Kneeling Assisted Cobra | Forward Bend with Crossed Legs | Pressing Head to Knees | Reverse Half Lotus with Leg Lift and Knee Press | Sitting Stool Assisted Bow Pose

Back

Lifting to a Seated Position | Thumb Press | Seated Side Back Bow with Foot Press | Stretching the Arm in the Triangle Position | Pull up with Spinal Twist | Butterfly Pullback into Knees | Arm Wraparound Pullback with Knee Press | Palm Press Back | Souider to Opposite Knee Spinal Twist

Back

Butterfly Twist | Kneel on the Back | Back Press | Roll With Forearm | Standing Cobra | Subscapular Release | Pressing the Back in the Side Position | Shaking the Legs

Lower Body

Butterfly

Lower Body

Rotating the Foot | Pulling & Cracking Each Toe | 3 Points Leg Pressing | Stretch and Press Medial Leg | Quadriceps Stretch | Press and Stretch Lateral Leg | Chest to Foot Pressing | Triangle Stretch | Palming the Feet Outside

Lower Body

Pressing the Outer Leg | Stretch Straight Leg | Pressing the Flexed Leg | Pressing Foot to Thigh | Knee Stretch with Hamstring Press | Stretching the Arched Foot | Stretching the Arched Foot | Raised Foot Leg Stretch | Back Backwrd Leg Lift

Lower Body

Leg Blood Stop | Z - Step | Hip Flex | Knee Compress with Knee Pullback | Push Legs Forward with Counterforce | Single Leg Locust | Rotating the Hips | Hamstring and Calf Stretch | Rolling Pin with Supported Posterior Leg

Lower Body

Palming the Feet Inside | Elbow Press | Lean Back Grasping | Reverse Half Lotus with Leg Press | Knee to Chest with Forearm Compression | Extend Foot Toward Head | Hip Stretch | Butterfly Hands Pressing in Tree Position | Vertical Leg Stretch

Lower Body

Pigeon Pose Press | Vertical Half Lotus Thigh Press | Pressing the Thigh & Pulling the Foot | Press Heels to Buttocks | Pressing the Leg in the Tree Position | Knee to Knee Hip Flex | Stretching the Crossed Leg Horizontally | Buttock Pressing | Standing feet to feet

Make your own circuit: **Circle and do your Top 5-10**

Block Exercises

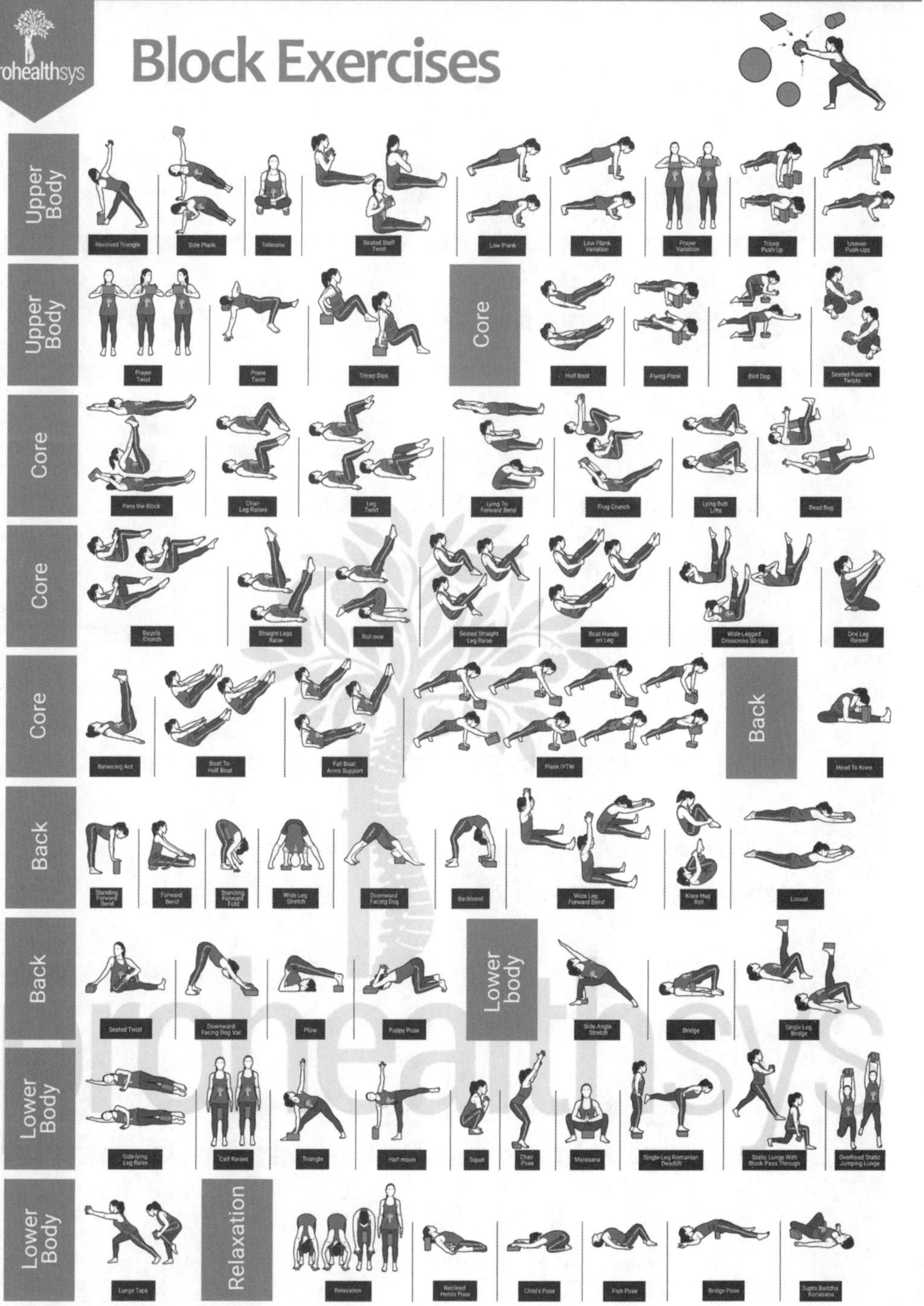

Upper Body
Revolved Triangle | Side Plank | Tolasana | Seated Staff Twist | Low Plank | Low Plank Variation | Prayer Variation | Tricep Push-Up | Uneven Push-Ups

Upper Body
Prayer Twist | Prone Twist | Tricep Dips

Core
Half Boat | Flying Plank | Bird Dog | Seated Russian Twists

Core
Pass the Block | Chair Leg Raises | Leg Twist | Lying To Forward Bend | Frog Crunch | Lying Butt Lifts | Dead Bug

Core
Bicycle Crunch | Straight Legs Raise | Roll over | Seated Straight Leg Raise | Boat Hands on Leg | Wide-Legged Crisscross Sit-Ups | One Leg Raised

Core
Balancing Act | Boat To Half Boat | Full Boat Arms Support | Plank IYTW

Back
Head To Knee

Back
Standing Forward Bend | Forward Bend | Standing Forward Fold | Wide Leg Stretch | Downward Facing Dog | Backbend | Wide Leg Forward Bend | Knee Hug Roll | Locust

Back
Seated Twist | Downward Facing Dog Var. | Plow | Puppy Pose

Lower body
Side Angle Stretch | Bridge | Single Leg Bridge

Lower Body
Side-lying Leg Raise | Calf Raises | Triangle | Half moon | Squat | Chair Pose | Malasana | Single-Leg Romanian Deadlift | Static Lunge With Block Pass Through | Overhead Static Jumping Lunge

Lower Body
Lunge Taps

Relaxation
Relaxation | Reclined Heros Pose | Child's Pose | Fish Pose | Bridge Pose | Supta Baddha Konasana

Physical activity has many health benefits and potential side effects, the creators are not responsible for injuries associated with using this poster. We will take partial credit for the health gains you will receive ☺
Consult a professional before you start, know your limit play within it. Breathe, do exercises on both sides of body for balance. Stop if you experience unexpected pain or discomfort

Make your own circuit: **Circle and do your Top 5**

SFMA and FMS Exercises

Upper Body

- Supine Cervical Extension
- C1-C2 Cervical Rotation
- Active Supine Cervical Rotation, 80- Degree
- Passive Cervical Rotation
- Active Supine Cervical Flexion, Chin to Chest
- Passive Supine Cervical Flexion
- Active Supine OA cervical Flexion, 20-Degree
- Cervical Pattern Three
- Cervical Pattern Two
- Cervical Pattern One

Upper Body

- Active Prone Upper Extremity Pattern Two
- Active Prone Upper Extremity Pattern One
- Passive Prone Upper Extremity Pattern One
- Passive Prone Upper Extremity Pattern Two
- Shoulder Mobility 1 Right
- Shoulder Mobility 2 Right
- Shoulder Mobility 3 Right
- Upper Extremity Pattern One
- Upper Extremity Pattern Two
- Active Scapular Stability
- Upper Extremity Provocation Pattern One
- Upper Extremity Provocation Pattern Two

Upper Body

- Supine Reciprocal Shoulder Pattern

Core

- Trunk Stability Pushup 1
- Trunk Stability Pushup 2
- Trunk Stability Pushup 3
- Rotary Stability 1
- Rotary Stability 2
- Rotary Stability 3

Back

- Single-Leg Backward Bend
- Backward Bend without Upper Extremity
- Unilateral Shoulder Backward Bend
- Single-Leg Forward Bend
- Multi-Segmental Rotation
- Multi-Segmental Extension
- Multi-Segmental Flexion
- Inline Lunge 3 Side View
- Inline Lunge 3 Front View
- Inline Lunge 2 Side View
- Inline Lunge 2 Front View
- Inline Lunge 1 Side View

Back

- Inline Lunge 1 Front View
- Spinal Extension Test
- Spinal Flexion Test
- Lumbar-Locked (ER) Extension/Rotation
- Long-Sitting Toe Touch
- Lumbar-Locked (IR) Passive Rotation/Extension
- Lumbar-Locked (IR) Active Rotation/Extension
- Seated Rotation
- Prone Press-Up

Back

- Prone on Elbow Rotation/Extension
- Supine Lat Stretch Hips Extended
- Prone Rocking

Lower Body

- Prone Passive Hip Extension
- Supine Knee-to-Chest
- Seated Active External Tibial Rotation
- Seated Active External Hip Rotation
- Seated Rotation

Lower Body

- Seated Active Internal Tibial Rotation
- Seated Passive External Hip Rotation
- Seated Passive Internal Hip Rotation
- Modified Thomas Test 1
- Modified Thomas Test 2
- Modified Thomas Test 3
- Modified Thomas
- Supine Lat Stretch Hips Flexed
- Passive Straight-Leg Raise

Lower Body

- Seated Active Internal Hip Rotation
- Prone Active Hip Extension
- Active Straight-Leg Raise
- Prone Active External Hip Rotation
- Prone Active Internal Hip Rotation
- Prone Passive External Hip Rotation
- Prone Passive Internal Hip Rotation
- Active Straight-Leg Raise 1
- Active Straight-Leg Raise 2
- Active Straight-Leg Raise 3
- Single-Leg Stance

Lower Body

- Hurdle Step 1 Side/Front View
- Hurdle Step 2 Side/Front View
- Hurdle Step 3 Side/Front View
- Deep Squat 1 Side/Front View
- Deep Squat 2 Side/Front View
- Deep Squat 3 Side/Front View
- Standing Hip Extension
- Overhead Deep Squat

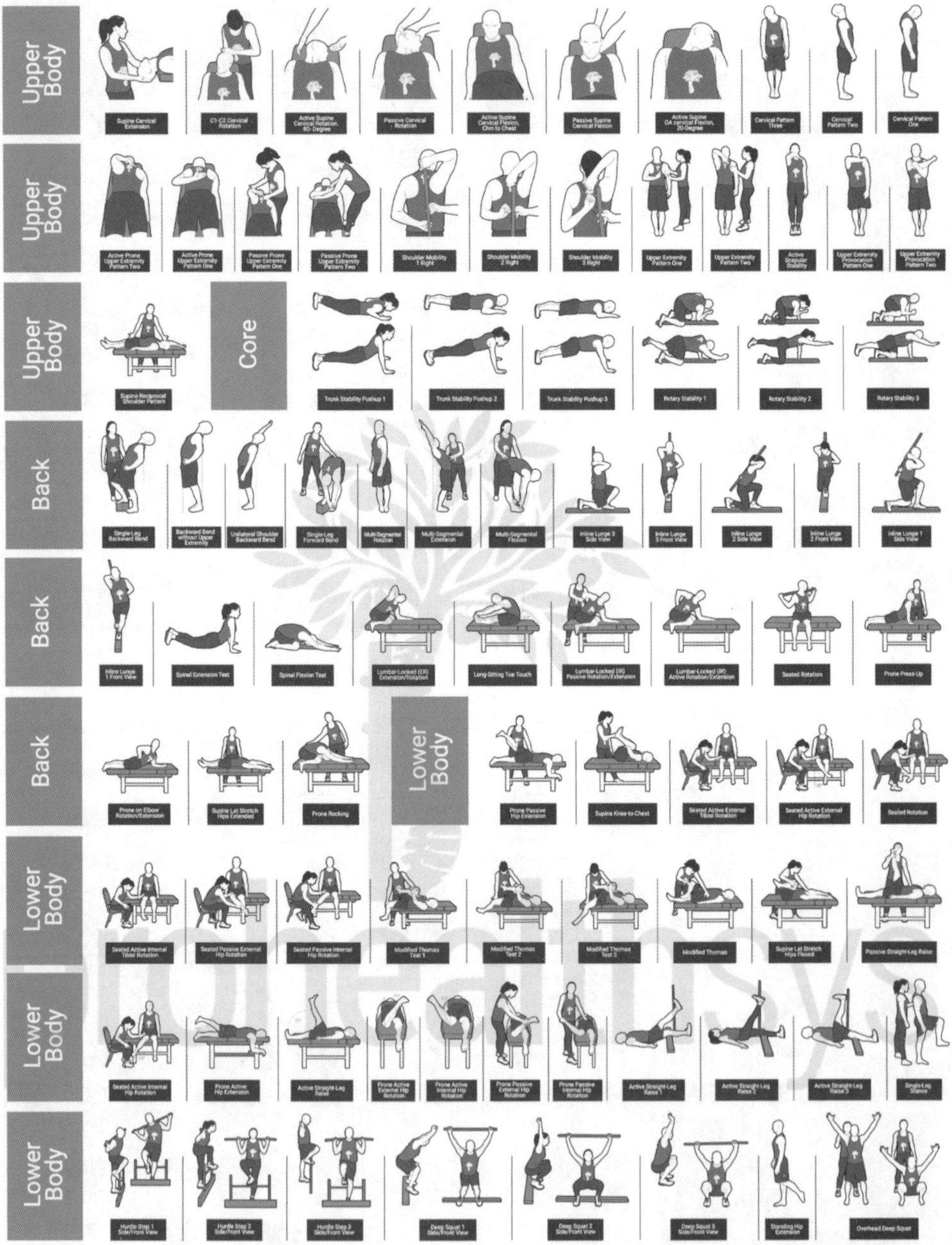

Physical activity has many health benefits and potential side effects; the creators are not responsible for injuries associated with using this poster. We will take partial credit for the health gains you will receive ☺
Consult a professional before you start, know your limit play within it. Breathe, do exercises on both sides of body for balance. Stop if you experience unexpected pain or discomfort.

prohealthsys

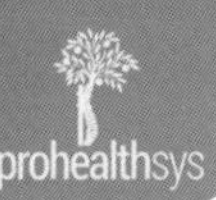

Yoga Exercises

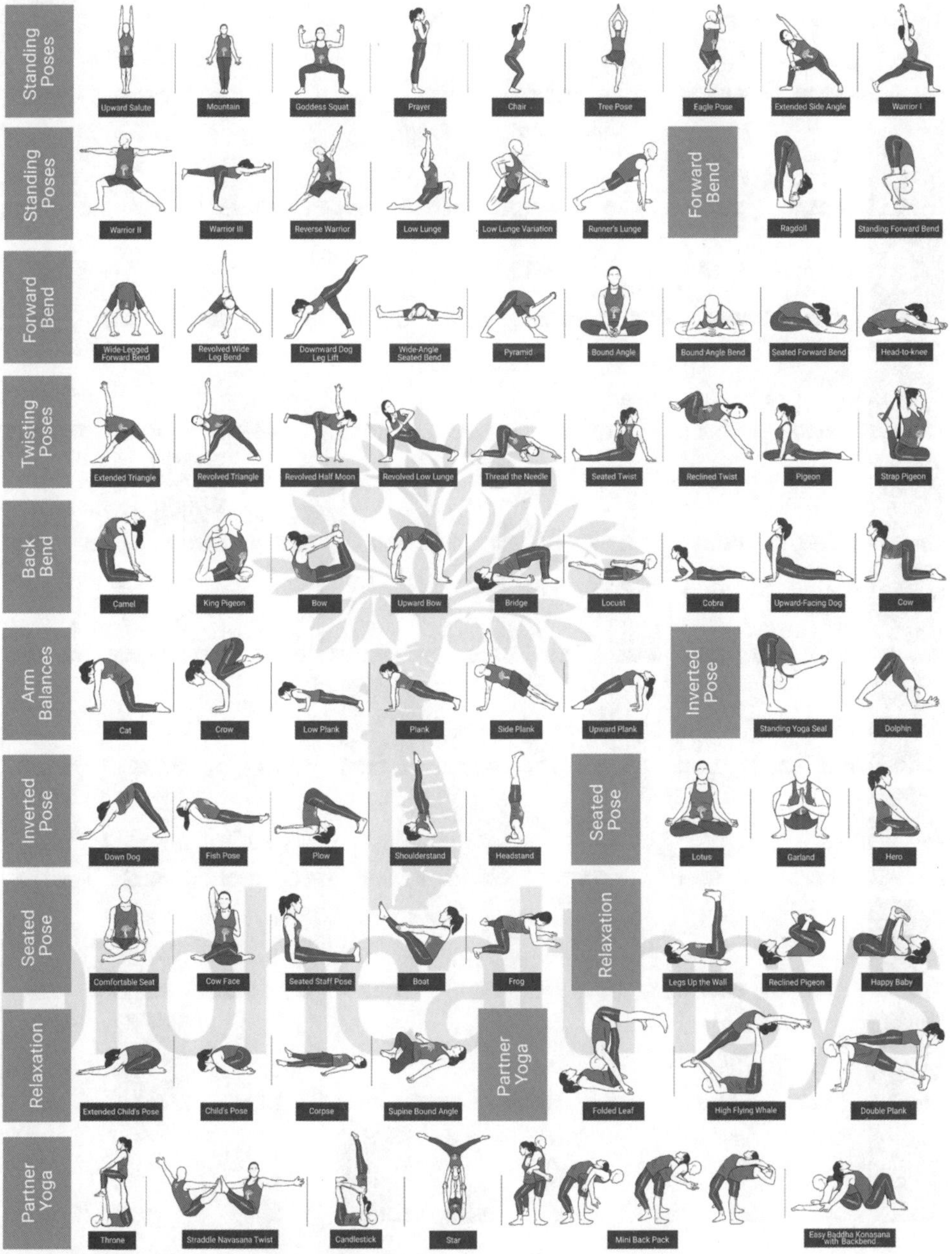
Standing Poses
Upward Salute
Mountain
Goddess Squat
Prayer
Chair
Tree Pose
Eagle Pose
Extended Side Angle
Warrior I
Standing Poses
Warrior II
Warrior III
Reverse Warrior
Low Lunge
Low Lunge Variation
Runner's Lunge
Forward Bend
Ragdoll
Standing Forward Bend
Forward Bend
Wide-Legged Forward Bend
Revolved Wide Leg Bend
Downward Dog Leg Lift
Wide-Angle Seated Bend
Pyramid
Bound Angle
Bound Angle Bend
Seated Forward Bend
Head-to-knee
Twisting Poses
Extended Triangle
Revolved Triangle
Revolved Half Moon
Revolved Low Lunge
Thread the Needle
Seated Twist
Reclined Twist
Pigeon
Strap Pigeon
Back Bend
Camel
King Pigeon
Bow
Upward Bow
Bridge
Locust
Cobra
Upward-Facing Dog
Cow
Arm Balances
Cat
Crow
Low Plank
Plank
Side Plank
Upward Plank
Inverted Pose
Standing Yoga Seal
Dolphin
Inverted Pose
Down Dog
Fish Pose
Plow
Shoulderstand
Headstand
Seated Pose
Lotus
Garland
Hero
Seated Pose
Comfortable Seat
Cow Face
Seated Staff Pose
Boat
Frog
Relaxation
Legs Up the Wall
Reclined Pigeon
Happy Baby
Relaxation
Extended Child's Pose
Child's Pose
Corpse
Supine Bound Angle
Partner Yoga
Folded Leaf
High Flying Whale
Double Plank
Partner Yoga
Throne
Straddle Navasana Twist
Candlestick
Star
Mini Back Pack
Easy Baddha Konasana with Backbend

Physical activity has many health benefits and potential side effects; the creators are not responsible for injuries associated with using this poster. We will take partial credit for the health gains you will receive ☺
Consult a professional before you start, know your limit play within it. Breathe, do exercises on both sides of body for balance. Stop if you experience unexpected pain or discomfort

Huge wall poster available

Make your own circuit: **Circle and do your Top 5-50**

prohealthsys

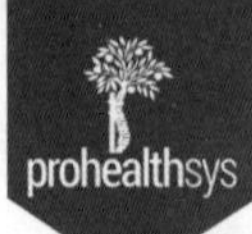

Sexercise

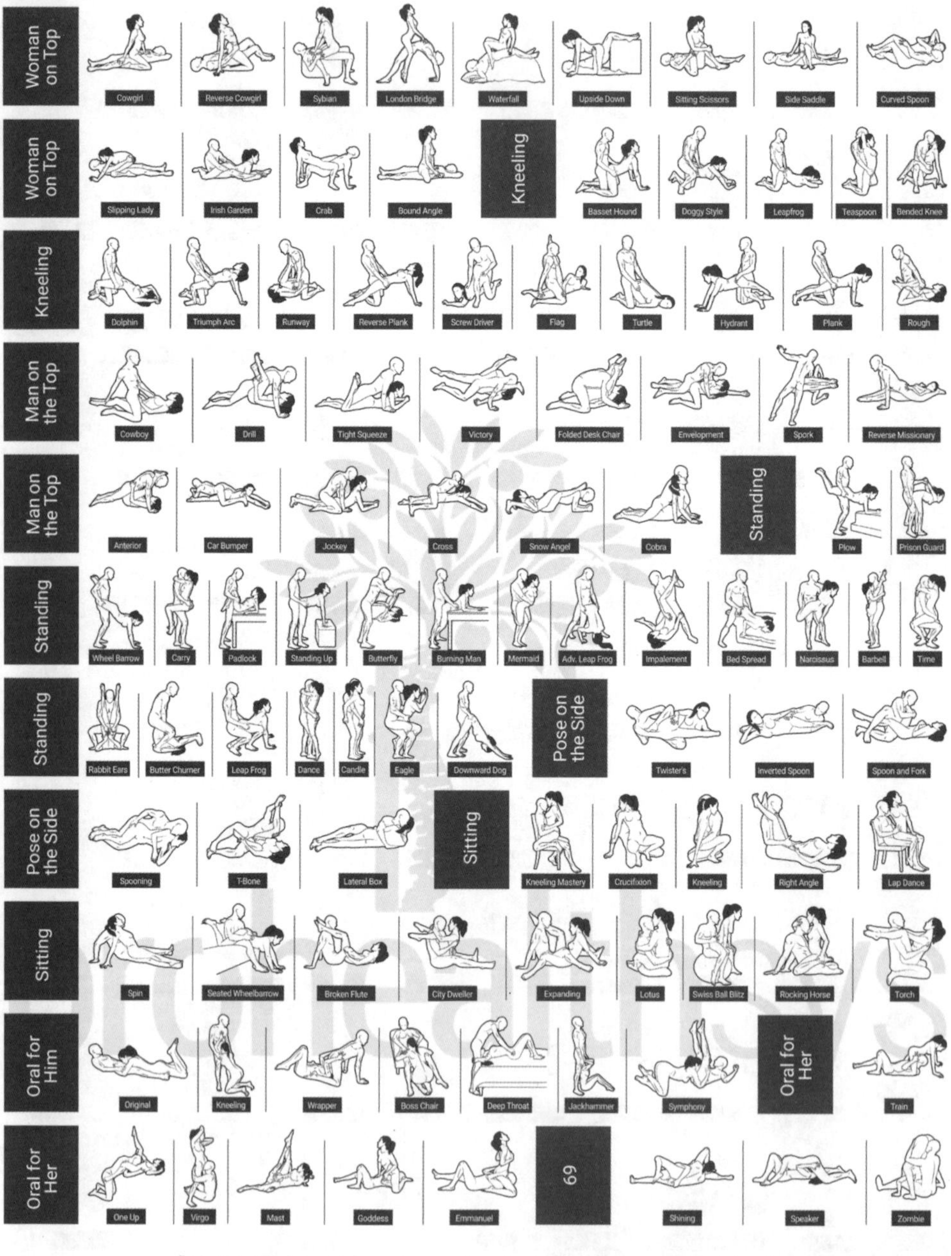

Woman on Top
Cowgirl
Reverse Cowgirl
Sybian
London Bridge
Waterfall
Upside Down
Sitting Scissors
Side Saddle
Curved Spoon
Woman on Top
Slipping Lady
Irish Garden
Crab
Bound Angle
Kneeling
Basset Hound
Doggy Style
Leapfrog
Teaspoon
Bended Knee
Kneeling
Dolphin
Triumph Arc
Runway
Reverse Plank
Screw Driver
Flag
Turtle
Hydrant
Plank
Rough
Man on the Top
Cowboy
Drill
Tight Squeeze
Victory
Folded Desk Chair
Envelopment
Spork
Reverse Missionary
Man on the Top
Anterior
Car Bumper
Jockey
Cross
Snow Angel
Cobra
Standing
Plow
Prison Guard
Standing
Wheel Barrow
Carry
Padlock
Standing Up
Butterfly
Burning Man
Mermaid
Adv. Leap Frog
Impalement
Bed Spread
Narcissus
Barbell
Time
Standing
Rabbit Ears
Butter Churner
Leap Frog
Dance
Candle
Eagle
Downward Dog
Pose on the Side
Twister's
Inverted Spoon
Spoon and Fork
Pose on the Side
Spooning
T-Bone
Lateral Box
Sitting
Kneeling Mastery
Crucifixion
Kneeling
Right Angle
Lap Dance
Sitting
Spin
Seated Wheelbarrow
Broken Flute
City Dweller
Expanding
Lotus
Swiss Ball Blitz
Rocking Horse
Torch
Oral for Him
Original
Kneeling
Wrapper
Boss Chair
Deep Throat
Jackhammer
Symphony
Oral for Her
Train
Oral for Her
One Up
Virgo
Mast
Goddess
Emmanuel
69
Shining
Speaker
Zombie

Physical activity has many health benefits and potential side effects; the creators are not responsible for injuries associated with using this poster. We will take partial credit for the health gains you will receive. Consult a professional before you start, know your limit play within it. Breathe, do exercises on both sides of body for balance. Stop if you experience unexpected pain or discomfort

Huge wall poster available

Make your own circuit: **Circle and do your Top 5-10**

Partner Exercises

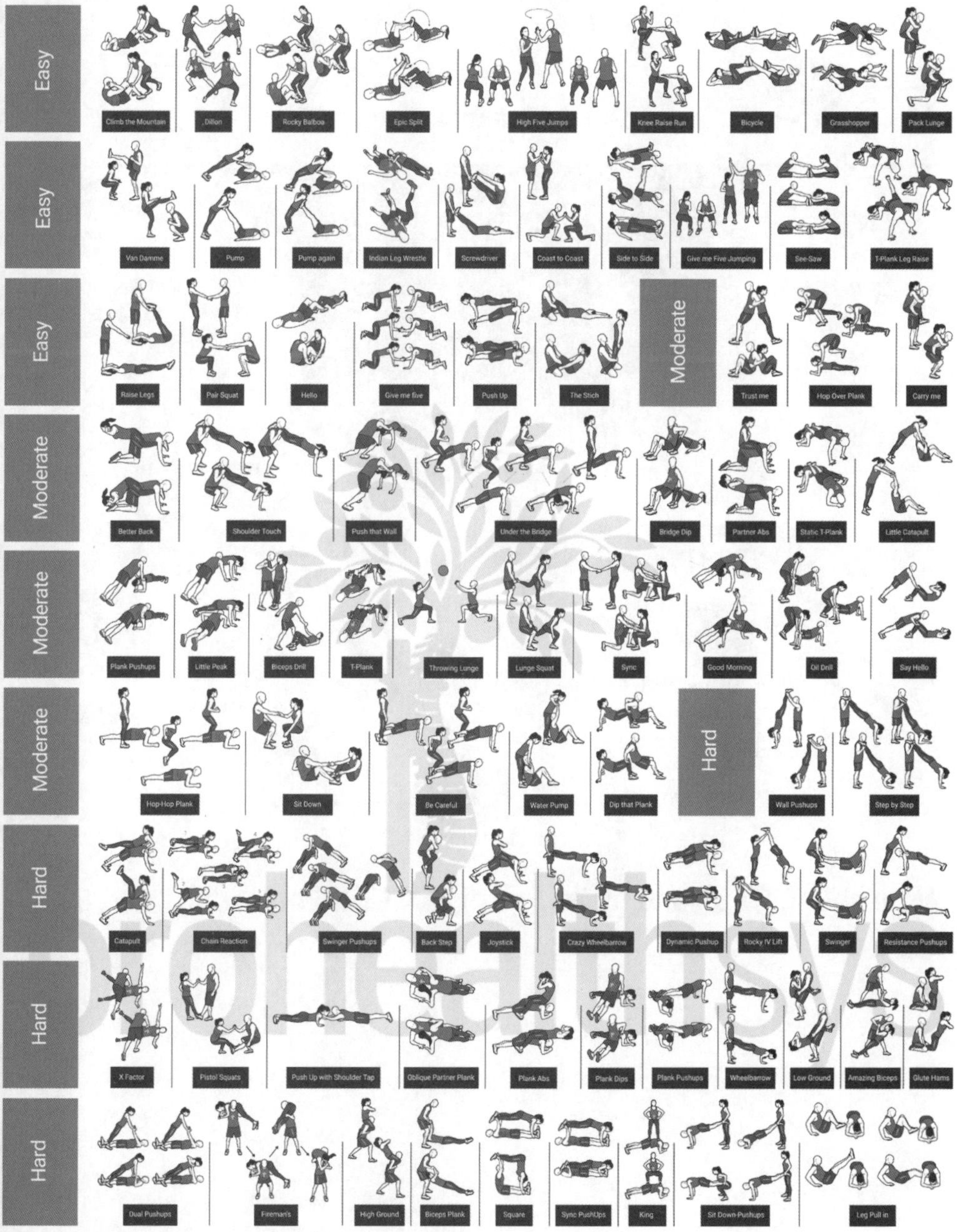

Easy

Climb the Mountain · Dillon · Rocky Balboa · Epic Split · High Five Jumps · Knee Raise Run · Bicycle · Grasshopper · Pack Lunge

Easy

Van Damme · Pump · Pump again · Indian Leg Wrestle · Screwdriver · Coast to Coast · Side to Side · Give me Five Jumping · See-Saw · T-Plank Leg Raise

Easy

Raise Legs · Pair Squat · Hello · Give me five · Push Up · The Stich

Moderate

Trust me · Hop Over Plank · Carry me

Moderate

Better Back · Shoulder Touch · Push that Wall · Under the Bridge · Bridge Dip · Partner Abs · Static T-Plank · Little Catapult

Moderate

Plank Pushups · Little Peak · Biceps Drill · T-Plank · Throwing Lunge · Lunge Squat · Sync · Good Morning · Oil Drill · Say Hello

Moderate

Hop-Hop Plank · Sit Down · Be Careful · Water Pump · Dip that Plank

Hard

Wall Pushups · Step by Step

Hard

Catapult · Chain Reaction · Swinger Pushups · Back Step · Joystick · Crazy Wheelbarrow · Dynamic Pushup · Rocky IV Lift · Swinger · Resistance Pushups

Hard

X Factor · Pistol Squats · Push Up with Shoulder Tap · Oblique Partner Plank · Plank Abs · Plank Dips · Plank Pushups · Wheelbarrow · Low Ground · Amazing Biceps · Glute Hams

Hard

Dual Pushups · Fireman's · High Ground · Biceps Plank · Square · Sync PushUps · King · Sit Down-Pushups · Leg Pull in

Write your GOALs and measures of SUCCESS here: